IMAGES OF WAR

The Germans in Flanders 1914

RARE PHOTOGRAPHS FROM WARTIME ARCHIVES

DAVID BILTON

'Flanders! The word is heard by everyone in the German Fatherland with a silent shudder, but also with just and intense pride. It was here that the British were made to realise that German heroism was not to be vanquished.'

Pen & Sword
MILITARY

First published in Great Britain in 2012 by
PEN & SWORD MILITARY
an imprint of
Pen & Sword Books Ltd
47 Church Street
Barnsley
South Yorkshire
S70 2AS

ISBN 978 1 84884 445 2

A CIP catalogue record for this book is available from the British Library

Typeset in Gill Sans by
Phoenix Typesetting, Auldgirth, Dumfriesshire

Printed and bound in England by
CPI UK

Pen & Sword Books Ltd incorporates the Imprints of Pen & Sword Aviation, Pen & Sword Family History, Pen & Sword Maritime, Pen & Sword Military, Pen & Sword Discovery, Wharncliffe Local History, Wharncliffe True Crime, Wharncliffe Transport, Pen & Sword Select, Pen & Sword Military Classics, Leo Cooper, The Praetorian Press, Remember When, Seaforth Publishing and Frontline Publishing

For a complete list of Pen & Sword titles please contact
PEN & SWORD BOOKS LIMITED
47 Church Street, Barnsley, South Yorkshire, S70 2AS, England
E-mail: enquiries@pen-and-sword.co.uk
Website: www.pen-and-sword.co.uk

Contents

Acknowledgements

When she found out I was writing another book, my younger daughter gave me a look that said it all. This book then turned into three. Sorry to everyone at home, and thanks.

As with previous books, a great big thank you to Anne Coulson for her help in checking the text and to The Prince Consort's Library for all their help.

Errors of omission or commission are mine alone.

Introduction

The purpose of these three books, The German Army in Flanders 1914, The German Army in Flanders 1915 and The German Army in Flanders 1916–1918, is not to analyse the strategic, tactical, political or economic reasons for the fighting in Flanders but rather to chronicle the events that happened there during that period. The brief words rely on the pictures to tell a large part of the story: pictures from a private collection; I also use texts (detailed in the bibliography) published during the period of this history. The books are not necessarily a chronological photographic record as some periods were more fully recorded than others; they are more an attempt to provide a cameo of the experiences of the German Army in Flanders during the Great War. For most of the time an army is not fighting, and the photographs portray life outside the trenches as well as in them.

The causes of the Great War have been dealt with at length in many books so all I have done on this topic is set the scene as a prelude to the remainder of the book. As this book concerns Flanders, I have mostly disregarded the early fighting in Walloon Belgium, concentrating on those aspects of the invasion that are central to the story of Flanders.

As with my earlier books on the German Army, I include a day-to-day chronology to show what was happening across the Belgian Flanders Front from the German point of

Many things remained unchanged despite the arrival of the German Army. Here, as throughout the years, Flemish women sit in the street embroidering linen, an old local skill.

A view of Brugge sent home by a soldier recovering in a field hospital in the city.

view. However, Flanders being a coastal area, I have included events at sea during the period as well as information about aerial activity as the Flanders coast was the closest occupied territory to the British mainland. Flanders was indeed a strategically important area, but not every day is listed; as on every other front during the war, some days were very active but most were no more or less significant than the previous one. For a missing day the GHQ report simply read: 'In Flanders today again only artillery activity' or 'In the West nothing new' – in English, the famous words: 'All quiet on the Western Front'.

The reality underlying the fact of this bland statement is revealed in the letters home of Lothar Dietz, a philosophy student from Leipzig, who was killed near Ypres on 15 April 1915. 'You at home can't have the faintest idea of what it means to us when in the newspaper it simply and blandly says: "In Flanders to-day again only artillery activity". Far better to go over the top in the most foolhardy attack, cost what it may, than stick it out all day long under shell-fire, wondering all the time whether the next one will maim one or blow one to bits'.

Ghent, a city well behind the lines, was used for rest and recovery and as a base for field hospitals. This card was sent by a member of *2 Marine Division.*

Flanders was an important area for naval offensive operations and had to be guarded against Entente naval attack and the possibility of naval-supported invasion. For this reason the sea-front was guarded by regiments of marine artillery. 'Thirty guns of the heaviest calibre had been set up there, among them five of 38 cm., four of 30.5 cm., and besides them a large number of quick-firing guns from 10.5 to 21 cm. calibre.' Manning these fortifications and the coastal trenches employed large numbers of men.

The Naval Corps, troops to defend the naval areas, was instituted under the leadership of Admiral von Schröder on September 3, 1914, and played a part in the taking of Antwerp on October 10, 1914. Naval Corps General Command had its headquarters at Bruges. The infantry of the Naval Corps consisted of three regiments of able seamen and marines. The latter in particular played a part in the great battles in Flanders in 1916 and 1917.

Similarly, taking the offensive to the Royal Navy required boats, aircraft and submarines. Torpedo-boat flotillas were based at Zeebrugge which was to be the scene of an attack by British Marines and the Royal Navy in April 1917. There were seaplane bases at Ostend and Zeebrugge; the facilities at the latter were used to overhaul U-boats for long distance work and as a base for short range submarines. The Naval Corps in Flanders had thirty-eight submarines at its disposal in 1917. As Allied planes often patrolled the coast, many submarines were based at Bruges and along the canal to the coast. A repair and building shipyard for the Flanders Naval forces was situated in Ghent.

Flanders is very difficult to define geographically; it has been in a continuous state of flux for hundreds of years. Originally covering a much larger area than today, what was Flanders during the war differed according to the army in which a soldier fought. To the Belgian army it was a defined area that covered the unconquered part of their nation and part of the conquered territory; to the French it was the area of Belgium that they were fighting in; to the British it covered their Front from just north of Arras in France to their furthest west boundary at Boesinghe, north of Ypres. For the German Army, the Flanders Front stretched from Dixmude in the north to Frelinghien in the south, opposite the area held by the French and the British, but, to the General Staff at OHL, Flanders also included

Multiple views of Zonnebeke sent by a Landwehr soldier in *45 Reserve Division*. This division fought in Belgium from the start of the war until sent to the Somme in 1916.

At Comines the border with France was just over the bridge.

the conquered coastal regions of Belgium defended by the Kaiserliche Marine, sea soldiers who guarded the coast and fought in the trenches. As this book is about the German Army, it is their geographical understanding of Flanders (Flandern) that has been used; activity in French Flanders is only mentioned in passing where it relates to the events in Belgium.

The most important town in the region, Ypres, was a focus for much of the fighting in the area. For the German Army its fall would allow them to continue through to the Channel Ports, depriving the British of the close entry points they needed to maintain their army in the field; for the British, once Ypres was secure, their focus of attack covered the whole of the Flanders Front.

Ypres lies in a basin formed by a maritime plain intersected by canals, and dominated on the north, north-east and south by low wooded hills. The canals, the Yser being the most important, follow a south-east to north-east direction; a number of streams flow in the same direction and there are three large ponds: Dickebusch, Zillebeke and Bellewaarde.

The hills that form the sides of the Ypres basin are very low and, at that time, were partly wooded. Their crests run through Houthulst Forest, Poelcapelle, Passchendaele, Broodseinde, Becelaere, Gheluvelt, Hill 60 and St. Eloi. Further south is the Messines-Wytschaete ridge, and to the south-west are the Hills of Flanders.

Houthulst Forest was the largest of the woods. Further south, after Westroosebeke, Passchendaele and Zonnebeke were other woods that were to become famous: Polygone, Nonne-Bosschen (Nonnes), Glencorse, Inverness and Herentage.

Surrounded by low hills, the numerous small waterways and the area's maritime climate gave the area around Ypres a character that was different to the rest of the front. The marshy ground, almost at sea level, is 'further sodden by constant rain and mists', forming a spongy mass that made it impossible to dig trenches or underground shelters. The water level is very near the surface, making parapets the only suitable and possible type of defence-works. Shell craters immediately filled with water and became death traps for the wounded, careless or unlucky. Such images create the iconography of the Flanders battles.

Menin Centre before the war.

The geology and geography of the area meant that both sides centred their defence 'around the woods, villages and numerous farms, which were converted into redoubts with concrete blockhouses and deep wire entanglements'. Any slight piece of higher ground was fiercely contested. The dominating hill crests 'were used as observation posts – the lowering sky being usually unfavourable for aerial observation – while their counter-slopes masked the concentrations of troops for the attacks.' As a result the fighting was at its most intense along the crests and around the fortified farms.

There had been considerable fighting in Belgium before Ypres became the focal point. The arrival of German troops was only transient and without bloodshed. 'According to local accounts, the first contact for the people of Ypres with the First World War was the arrival of thousands of German troops on 7th October 1914.' These were cavalry and cyclists on their way north, who informed the Burgomaster that they would be there for three days. 'They began to enter the town from the south-east along the road from Menin through the Menin Gate (Menenpoort) and from the south through the Lille Gate (Rijselpoort). Scouting parties advanced north and west beyond Ypres in the directions of Boesinghe, Vlamertinghe and Elverdinghe. By 9pm the town, its streets and market square were packed full of horses and riders, soldiers, carts, carriages, cars, field kitchens and guns.' The exact number of troops is unknown but local accounts reckon about 10,000. 'Soldiers were billeted for the night in the halls of the Cloth Hall, in schools, the army barracks, the waiting rooms at the railway station and in houses with the local people. The mayor, Mr Colaert, advised the people of Ypres to stay calm and remain in their homes.'

'The shops were crammed full of German soldiers. By way of payment some offered German coins, others had paper notes. Some gave pre-printed coupons to the shop-keepers or locals for food and clothes. There were stories of damage to the railway station, stealing from local people's homes, and drinking. The bakers were ordered to have 8,000 bread rolls baked and ready for 8.30am the next morning, 8th October, to distribute to the troops. Hay, straw and oats were requisitioned and the town's coffers were emptied of 62,000 Francs.' According to one account the demand was for 70,000

Blankenberghe
La rue et rampe Malécot

Blankenberghe town centre before the war. According to the 1911 Encyclopaedia Brittanica BLANKENBERGHE was a 'seaside watering-place on the North Sea in the province of West Flanders, Belgium, 12 m. N.E. of Ostend, and about 9 m. N.W. of Bruges, with which it is connected by railway. It is more bracing than Ostend, and has a fine parade over a mile in length. During the season, which extends from June to September, it receives a large number of visitors, probably over 60,000 altogether, from Germany as well as from Belgium. There is a small fishing port as well as a considerable fishing-fleet. Two miles north of this place along the dunes is Zeebrugge, the point at which the new ship-canal from Bruges enters the North Sea. Fixed population (1904) 5925.'

francs, 5,000 more than was available. 'Horses and wagons were requisitioned and paid for with coupons. Anyone in receipt of a coupon as payment was, however, unlikely ever to receive payment from the German Army because the next day, 8th October, the Germans started to move out of the town from about midday. The soldiers on foot went in the direction of Dickebusch. The cavalry went in the direction of Vlamertinghe. They were never to return.'

Ypres had been a populous town in the Middle Ages but by 1914 numbered less than 17,000 occupants. Its commerce was based around the manufacture of flax, lace, ribbons, cotton and soap. It was a minor tourist area because of its medieval Cloth Hall, the largest non-religious Gothic building in Europe. The newly arrived British troops found it to be 'a gem of a town with its lovely old-world gabled houses, red-tiled roofs, and no facto-ries visible to spoil the charm.'

The OHL history described why the area was so heavily contested. The possession of Ypres to the English was a point of honour. For both sides it was the central pivot of operations. From the time artillery fire could reach the town, it became a legitimate target for German gunners because it lay so close to the front that the German advance could be seen from its towers – so claimed the OHL history of the battle. It also concealed enemy batteries and sheltered their reserves. Captain Schwink wrote in 1917 that 'for the sake of our troops we had to bring it under fire; for German life is more precious than the finest Gothic architecture.'

The Ypres salient was key to the fighting on the front which can be divided into three major battles known to the British as First, Second and Third Ypres, but there were many smaller battles between the major offensives. The first battle was a result of a powerful German offensive – a counter-stroke to the battles of the Yser – then an attempt to take Ypres; during this battle arose the myth of the students valiantly storming the British defences. 'The second stage was marked by British and Franco-British offensives, begun in the second half of 1916 and considerably developed during the summer and autumn of the following year.' Ending in November 1917 in a sea of mud, these battles eventually achieved their aim – moving the Ypres Salient eastwards and opening the Flanders plains. During the German offensives of April 1918, British positions to the south of Ypres were attacked but did not fall, and in September and October of the same year the positions held in Flanders were evacuated.

Of the hundreds of thousands of men who served in Flanders, one stands out for special note – Adolf Hitler. As a volunteer, he served throughout the war with *16 Bavarian Reserve Infantry Regiment,* in *6 Bavarian Reserve Division.* After being involved in the 1914 Ypres battles, the division was never again used in a lead assault role, becoming a static front-holding division, good in defence. There was a sound military reason for its not remaining an attack division: 'Its recruits were hardly the *crème de la crème* of German manhood, rather a motley assortment of callow youths and not always young, or fit, men from a range of backgrounds.' Hitler's unit was thrown into the Ypres offensive with heavy casualties – twenty per cent of the total casualties for the war in their first action. By November the regiment was down to one-third of its combat strength and Hitler had been awarded the Iron Cross 2nd Class.

As this book is written from the German point of view, it does not always fit in with the standard British view of events. Where possible I have merged both accounts to make one, but the difference between them is often quite surprising. Langemarck is possibly the most famous battle of First Ypres. The battle area viewed through opposing eyes is completely different.

To the British their 'defences around Ypres were at best, short disconnected lengths of trenches, three feet deep. Hastily constructed…they were without wire, dug-outs or communication trenches, and lacked anything in the nature of a second line.' Yet to the

The centre of Ypres in late November 1914 showing what is left of the Cloth Hall and belfry.

writers of the OHL book, 'Ypres', they were of considerable strength. 'On the morning of the 22nd a strong position lay to our immediate front. It followed a line Bixschoote-Langemarck-Zonnebeke-Reutel-Gheluvelt, and the I. and IV. British as well as the French IX. Corps, all picked troops, had been located there. They had dug a well-planned maze of trenches behind barbed wire entanglements.'

The confusion of war is also clearly shown at Langemarck. In the OHL book, 'Ypres', it is claimed that *209* and *212 Reserve Infantry Regiments* 'took Bixschoote from the British, after furious hand-to-hand fighting at 5.30.M., but then evacuated it in the night owing to an order being misunderstood.' The attacking troops left before their relief had arrived and as a result the enemy advanced into the evacuated village. The German writers were clear it was the British whom they fought but the British insist it was the French who held the village, their own positions being behind Bixschoote, at Steenstraat. Similarly the British claim that they had evacuated Poezelhoek Château on 31 October but the German account records that it was taken on 1 November after a heavy fight; again the Germans claim that they took Messines on 1 November after fierce street fighting that lasted throughout the day, while the British

Although Ypres was never captured, many German soldiers sent home postcards with views of the city. This card was sent by a soldier in *51 Reserve Division.*

reported it evacuated by 0800 hours.

The Flanders fighting of 1914 gave rise to the lasting legend of Langemarck. On 22 October, newly formed reserve infantry regiments, composed of young volunteer soldiers, sang patriotic songs as they attacked British positions. They were killed in their hundreds. In the official communiqué, the troops sang 'Deutschland, Deutschland über Alles' but the regimental history written after the war stated that the song was 'Die Wacht am Rhein'. While the official version suggested the singing was inspired by patriotism, the regimental reason was more mundane. As the unit wore Landsturm caps rather than pickelhaubes, the song was sung to identify the unit as German — they had previously been mistaken for British troops. Many of the regimental histories indicate that, during this period, it was common practice for men to sing, and it was often done simply to prevent friendly fire casualties.

Writing the OHL history of Ypres 1914, Captain Schwink explained why the fighting

Ypres at the end of the war: little was left undamaged. By the late 1960s, it was restored to what it had been in 1914.

was so hard and prolonged in Flanders. He blamed the war on the British and also noted how a hatred of the British kept the troops fighting. 'Hate of the British who were so jealous of us, who brought on the war for the sake of their money-bags and spread the conflagration all over the world, who at first hoped that it would be but necessary to pour out their silver bullets to annihilate Germany: all this steeled the hearts of our warriors in Flanders, whose creed was the justice of the German cause.'

A common misconception is that Second Ypres saw the first use of gas in warfare. Not only was it not the first use, but it was also not the first time on the Western Front. 'The French had fired primitive ethyl bromo-acetate rifle projectiles (*cartouches suffocantes*) as early as 1914 and stepped up their use in the Argonne sector in March 1915.' In April they introduced a chemical hand grenade, the 'Bertrand No.1'. Gas had also been used on the Eastern Front in January of the same year, when German artillery had fired around 18,000 xylyl bromide shells against the Russians during the Battle of Bomilow. Due to the sub-zero weather, its use had not been a success and, for reasons that remain unclear, the Russians did not inform their western allies that they had been shelled with gas.

The Christmas Truce of 1914 occurred along the Flanders Front. Here, over a period of a few days and nights hostilities gradually thawed, against higher authorities' wishes, and 25 December became a day of peace and even goodwill. Men from both sides joined each other in no-man's land to exchange tokens, talk and even play football.

Throughout the book German units are identified by italics and British and French troops by standard lettering.

1914 –
The Advance through Belgium

On 25 July the Austro-Hungarian populace were informed of the partial mobilisation of the army and Landsturm. By the end of the month Emperor Wilhelm had stated in an Imperial Ordnance that, apart from Bavaria, the German Empire was in a condition of war. This was not a state of war but a warning to the country that there could be a war. The next day the Emperor mobilised the army and Navy making 2 August the first day of mobilisation. Then, informing the German people that the country was being forced into war, he called upon all who were capable of bearing arms to defend the Fatherland.

At the beginning of the war the intentions of the French and Russians were unknown; the worst scenario was a more-or-less coordinated Franco-Russian attack. In the east, even facing only active service troops, the odds would be two to one in favour of the Russians, and the arrival of Far Eastern units and the reserves would lengthen the odds considerably. The Austro-Hungarians would also be in the same position.

Intelligence was aware of the Franco-Russian agreement to launch simultaneous attacks on the fifteenth day of mobilisation. As Russia had begun its mobilisation on 30 July this joint attack would be on 14 August. Troops would have to be transferred to the east by day thirteen of Russian mobilisation.

'While Austria and Germany prepared and mobilised, so too did the armies of France, Russia, Belgium and Britain. On 2 August, the French accused the Germans of crossing the frontier at three different points, shooting at the border personnel, stealing horses and killing a soldier. The next day, the German Ambassador in France, in his farewell letter, accused the French of violating Belgian territory and dropping bombs on Germany, giving his reason for leaving as the state of war that now existed between France and Germany. The die was cast – Europe would go to war.'

'Over 11,000 trains carried the army to the offensive.' In

Posted a year after the war started; a patriotic card sold on behalf of the Red Cross. 'For Emperor and Empire' reads the banner.

The easy way to arrive. A troop train arriving in Belgium in October 1914.

just over two weeks 2,150 trains crossed the Hohenzollern Bridge in Cologne – a train every ten minutes. Nearly four million men were mobilised, assembled and deployed, along with 850,000 horses.

Even before mobilisation had officially started, *16 Infantry Division* had moved into Luxembourg. A belated call from the Kaiser failed to halt the attack which was already underway by one company. By then, Lt. Feldmann and his men had successfully taken their objective, Troisvierges station, without control of which it would be more difficult for troops to access France. As a result, the next day, *Fourth Army* occupied the country. On 3 August, the Belgian government refused the German army entry and, from that point on, considered itself to be at war with Germany. The next day German forces crossed the frontier, meeting little opposition.

To many a new era in German history was beginning. There was 'a single great feeling of moral elevation…an ascent of a whole people to the heights'. In the crowd celebrating

Any suitable wagon was used to transport men to the front. In the early days of the war they were often covered in comments or messages.

Soldiers of *102 Infantry Regiment* in May 1914. Within four months they would have fought at Dinant and Namur before fighting on the Aisne and the Marne.

in Munich, a young Austrian fell down on his knees and thanked heaven for granting him the good fortune of 'being permitted to live at this time'. With him were thousands of others thinking similar thoughts, but the country did not share a unified experience. In Germany 'anxiety was as widespread as jubilation'.

On 4 August, Bethmann Hollweg told the Reichstag: 'We have been forced to ignore the just protestations of Luxembourg and the Belgian government. We shall make amends for this injustice as soon as our military goal is accomplished.' The action was justified because the French were already in Belgium trying to enter Germany in disguise. At the same time the French were warned that franc-tireurs would be shot.

That day, in the oppressive heat, 'cavalry with their field artillery and machine gun sections, trotted through the well cultivated, rolling land of East Belgium.' All ranks 'looked expectantly for the enemy at every hill…and every bend in the road.' After crossing the frontier 'notices were distributed everywhere among the population giving

From the start of the campaign in Belgium orders were issued about the consequences of non-compliance to German authority. Many people were shot because of the actions of real or imagined franc-tireurs. Priests were treated with distrust by advancing troops and many were shot for assisting the franc-tireurs. Here a Belgian priest, already decorated, is leaving for the war.

German soldiers defending themselves against franc-tireurs.

the reasons for our entrance and urgently warning them against making any resistance.'

As *2 Cavalry Corps* advanced, they encountered numerous instances of civilian resistance, so much so that it could only have been 'organized and planned by the Belgian Government'. As well as ordinary civilians, clergy took an active part. They cited numerous examples in their regimental history. 'Bicyclists, who came in the path of the column, hurried ahead to the next village and announced our advance. Prearranged signals such as unusual activity of the windmills, the display of flags on church towers, the ringing of bells and the burning of straw piles, announced our advance far and wide'.

Such knowledge gave the franc-tireurs time to prepare a reception. 'From strips of woodland and from houses, the roofs of which were provided with portholes by the removal of tiles and beams, yes, even from the church towers, the enemy was firing, especially at scouts and patrols, and many a good cavalryman here became the victim of the bullet of a cowardly assassin in ambush.'

As well as having continual problems with franc-tireurs, the cavalry also found the Belgians to be ungentlemanly in their conduct. When they sent a car into St. Trond, containing three men under the protection of the white flag, to demand the surrender of the town, it was fired upon. The officer was wounded five times and the other men were seriously wounded.

 'Between 3 and 20 August the German *Second Army's* special task force of 30,000 soldiers commanded by General Otto von Emmich crossed the border between the Ardennes and the Maastricht Appendix, a narrow strip of land between Holland and the heavily wooded and hilly area of eastern Belgium. Before them lay a formidable barrier: the Belgian fortress of Liège, one of the strongest in Europe, guarded by a belt of twelve concrete and steel forts.'

A night attack on 5/6 August penetrated the outer layer of Liège's forts and on 8 August Ludendorff took command of the 14th Brigade. After an all-night street battle, he entered the inner city. After the war Ludendorff wrote about his experiences of the battle, a battle that many of the officers thought had little chance of success. The first problem was finding their way to the defending Belgians in the pitch darkness. They were out of touch

Eight comrades from infantry regiment *Colbergsches-Grenadier-Regiment Graf Gneisenau (2. Pommersches) Nr. 9 of 3 Infantry Division* pose to celebrate their part in 1914 campaign in Belgium.

with the advance party and then took a wrong turn. Ludendorff was at the head of his men: 'We were immediately fired at, and the men fell right and left. I shall never forget hearing the thud of bullets striking human bodies.' After a few attacks on the Belgian defenders whose firing grew more intense, Ludendorff gave the order, as his men got closer, to retire and skirt round the position.

He then came upon a heap of dead and wounded German soldiers who were part of the advance party. After taking the machine gun position they were able to move on, but were soon engaged in heavy hand-to-hand fighting. Bringing up field howitzers cleared the opposition, and the advance continued although the troops were reluctant to move on further than the village. It then became apparent that they were inside the circle of the forts and cut off from any form of help.

After a cold night, Ludendorff, after a discussion with General von Emmich, continued the advance into the town. 'As we entered, many Belgian soldiers who were standing

Each side needed to score propaganda victories whenever it could to justify the war. This is a French card showing a Belgian soldier in front of the destruction caused by the German Army as it went through Haelen a few miles from the border with Germany.

about surrendered. Thinking that Colonel von Oven was in possession of the citadel, I went there with the brigade adjutant in a Belgian car which I had commandeered. When I arrived no German soldier was to be seen and the citadel was still in the hands of the enemy. I banged on the gates, which were locked. They were opened from inside. The few hundred Belgians who were there surrendered at my summons. The brigade now came up and took possession of the citadel, which I immediately put in a state of defence.'

Admiral von Müller, chief of the naval cabinet during the war, recorded in his diary on 8 August that Liège had fallen and the Kaiser was overjoyed at the news. It was also suggested that the navy attack the British naval ships protecting the transport of troops to Flanders, but the plan never materialised.

The first cavalry action of the war was fought between the investing and surrender of Liège. On 12 August a division of Belgian cavalry, assisted by engineers and cyclists, held the Haelen bridge against repeated attack. Known as the 'Battle of the Silver Helmets', De Witte's troops repulsed von der Marwitz's cavalry, despite numerous attempts to take the bridge using sabres and lances. Belgian losses were around 500 while the Germans lost 150 dead, 600 wounded and between 200-300 prisoners.

The *Cavalry Corps* history described the battle at some length, emphasising their losses in men and horses and how hard the battle had been fought. The story of the attack is one of bravery and loss: 'The commander (from *17 Dragoon Regiment)*, Captain Count Kalmein, led his squadron with great bravery and fell at the head of his valorous men. From this squadron, as also from 2nd squadron, only thirteen dismounted troopers returned. All officers, and all the other men were either killed, wounded, or captured.' The story was the same with *Cuirassier Regiment Königin*. 'Twice the enemy machine guns opened fire. Captain v. Horn, Commander of the 2nd squadron, fell, severely wounded. Only a few, under Lieutenant v. Ploetz, got as far as the enemy positions between the wire fences and hedges of Tuillerie Farm, and fewer still returned from there.' After reassembling, the losses were six officers, seventy one men and 270 horses. The heavy losses in men and horses were caused by 'extremely hot infantry and machine gun fire coming from ravines, ditches and hedges which were protected by wire'. It showed them that modern fire positions could not be successfully attacked by mounted troops.

A Belgian postcard showing Belgian troops readying themselves for combat. The card was sent to Schleswig-Holstein just before Christmas 1917 by a soldier serving in Brussels.

Armée belge   En présence de l'ennemi.

A photograph of the advance through Belgium taken by an inhabitant of the town. The troops march through on their way to the next battle.

Liège formally surrendered, two days behind Schlieffen's timetable, on 16 August, after its defensive cupolas had been systematically reduced by four batteries of 305mm Austrian howitzers. This allowed *First* and *Second Armies* to pass through the Liège corridor. Once through, they crossed the River Meuse and headed towards Mons and France. The Belgian Army rapidly dispersed. 'Brussels was occupied on 20 August and King Albert invested at Antwerp. But the Belgians demolished their communications infrastructure as they retreated. By mid-September all 26,000 railroad personnel of the German Army were engaged in trying to repair damaged Belgian lines, water towers, bridges, and tunnels'.

Whilst German troops marched through Belgium with a force of twelve corps and three cavalry divisions, they expected the French to attack into Lorraine, or into Lorraine and the Ardennes simultaneously. However on 7 August the French Army launched only a corps-sized attack towards Mühlhausen in the upper Alsace; but, on 14 August, in conformity to their agreement with the Russians, they began their offensive with two armies into Lorraine.

In the meantime the Belgian Army had

A card to justify the mass destruction of Louvain – franc-tireurs were everywhere.

The neat and ordered soldiers' cemetery at Barchon. Interred are the dead of *Infantry Regiments 25* and *53* who fell during the Lüttich battle.

mobilised around 100,000 men to defend their country; the pre-war conscription level had been very low, so low that German troops were surprised to find so many men of military age wandering about. 'On 4 August the Belgian government sent a note to the British and French governments, announcing that it would co-operate with them to resist the Germans' with the aim of guaranteeing the maintenance in future of Belgian sovereignty and independence.

According to one historian, the Germans met with little opposition from the Belgian Army but with considerable resistance from the civilian population, even when their army was nowhere to be seen. 'German bivouacs were frequently fired upon, and German cavalry was often ambushed' and most regiments reported some level of attack by Belgian civilians. Belgians caught with weapons in their hands were tried by court martial and shot. In spite of the potential punishment, the franc-tireurs were so successful that most units spent the nights in the open where it was easier to maintain security.

So deep was the fear of franc-tireurs that patrols skirted around villages and stayed off roads. According to reports many Belgian soldiers wore civilian clothes under their uniform to avoid capture and to enable them to become franc-tireurs.

The cavalry in particular complained of this form of warfare. Their patrols were fired upon and their wounded mistreated in a 'most cruel manner.'

In his memoirs, General Ludendorff commented at length on the problem of franc-tireurs and why such extreme countermeasures were needed. Having set up his first campaign headquarters in an inn at Hervé in Belgium, a town as yet undamaged by the war, he was woken during the night by brisk firing, some of which was directed at the inn. 'The franc-tireur warfare in Belgium had begun. It broke out everywhere the next day, and it was the sort of thing which aroused that intense bitterness that during those first years characterized the war on the Western front'.

Ludendorff blamed the Belgian government: 'It had systematically organized civilian warfare. The Garde Civique, which in days of peace had its own arms and special uniforms, were able to appear sometimes in one garb and sometimes in another. The Belgian soldiers must also have had a special civilian suit in their knapsacks at the commencement of the war. In the trenches near Fort Barchon, to the north-east of Liège, I myself saw uniforms which had been left behind by soldiers who had fought there.'

To Ludendorff, the actions of franc-tireurs went against the rules of war. If innocent people suffered because of their actions, they were responsible for the reprisals. The Belgian government was completely responsible for the situation.

The High Command's concern about potential problems with civilians is clearly shown by the order issued at Aix-La-Chapelle on 10 August, by Von Quast, Commanding *IX. Army Corps*. 'To protect ourselves from the extremely hostile attitude of the Belgian population it is necessary to take very vigorous and energetic measures against non-combatants who take part in the struggle. For this purpose no firearms or explosives must be retained by them'. The order then detailed how this was to be achieved. 'It is therefore ordered that before a locality is occupied a detachment of all arms will march in ahead of the columns and warn the population through the mayor and local clergy to deliver up all arms, ammunition, and explosive'.

The arms collected were to be destroyed and the explosives thrown into water. When summoned to surrender their arms and explosives, they were to be warned of the consequences. Non-compliance would be severely punished. 'After they have handed over their arms the inhabitants will be collected outside the locality, and the houses and gardens will be searched. If any arms are found, hostages will be executed and the place set on fire.' Similarly spies were to be shot and the houses where shooting took place were to be burned down.

Hostages were also taken during an over-night stay to guarantee the safety of the troops. Walter Bloem arrived at the village of Bloer which he felt was an ideal place for an ambush. His commanding officer gave orders to take a hostage from every household and to hold them overnight. As the night had been without incident, the next day they were released.

A Saxon officer, who was travelling through the Walloon area of Belgium, witnessed at first-hand what happened when franc-tireur activity was suspected. 'After Merlemont, we passed the village of Villers-en-Fague, which was burning. On the road lay the corpses

Two of the local children pose for a German photographer.

Diest Street in Louvain showing the randomness of the destruction.

of two grenadiers of the Guard. The population had informed the French of the grenadiers' approach by means of a signal given from the church tower. Enemy artillery had fired a few shrapnels at the tower, wounding or killing several grenadiers, where-upon our hussars had set the village afire. The priest and other inhabitants were shot.'

After his first experience of battle, Captain Bloem found that not all priests incited hatred against the invaders. After billeting his men he went to the house the staff were to use overnight. Dead tired, all he wanted to do was sleep. He knocked and the door was opened by an old priest who invited Bloem in. In one hand the priest carried a flick-ering candle with a bottle and two glasses under the other arm. 'He put the candle on the floor and poured, with a rather shaky hand, the gleaming red wine into the glasses, offered me one and held the other towards me.' The priest welcomed him into his home: '"Your good health, captain, and welcome to the simple home of a poor parish priest".'

The soldiers with Bloem found this kindness too much to believe. Recalling the stories of priests who led their parishioners in treacherous ambushes and provided troops with poisoned drinks, they implored him not to drink it. But relying on his own judgement, he clinked glasses and drank it down in one.

Regimental histories suggest that the civilian resistance was greater in the French-speaking Walloon districts than in the Flemish zone, where troops and civilians were able to co-exist, partly because of a basic commonality of language. In some cases the rela-tionship was very cordial as Jäger-battalion 3 found on 21 August in Nefelle. 'The local girls engaged the Jäger in conversation and fed them various delicacies, to the joy of the Jäger and their commander'. Money also helped the relationships, the troops going shop-ping whenever they could and so helping local businesses.

In his book 'The Advance from Mons, 1914', Walter Bloem recalled the difference between the two ethnic regions of Belgium. After passing through a village that had been razed to the ground for the shooting of troops by Belgian civilians, his unit passed through an area where the civilians appeared unworried and no one shot at them. When he spoke to them he understood their replies. It suddenly dawned on him that he was in the Flemish-speaking part of Belgium. Here he noted that the 'expression of hatred and

Abtransport gefangener Franzosen.

French POWs under guard as they are escorted towards the waiting transport that will take them from Flanders.

suspicion on every face had gone, and when questioned they replied fearlessly and at their ease.'

Even though the war was only a few weeks old, the supply train could not keep up and so the men received no bread or mail. Bloem's grenadiers who marched miles every day let him know how they felt. They had flour but no yeast and no time to bake. '"We get no bread, sir, and without bread no man can carry on like this for long – anyway if he has to slog along twenty to thirty miles every day".' Then there was the lack of mail: '"Having no bread is bad enough, sir, but having no post is ten times worse".'

'On 25 August nervous German troops set fire to the centre of Louvain, destroying 1000 houses, the Cathedral of St Pierre, and the University's library. Throughout Belgium between 5,000 and 6,000 citizens were summarily executed as suspected spies or saboteurs. Allied charges about the barbarity of the Huns were not long in coming.'

Spying was a matter that concerned both sides. An interrogated prisoner told his British

A charity card showing Crown Prince Wilhelm, successor to the German throne. Wilhelm had 'little command experience when he was named commander of the 5th Army in August 1914, shortly after the outbreak of World War I. In November 1914 William gave his first interview to a foreign correspondent and the first statement to the press made by a German noble since the outbreak of war. He said this in English:

"Undoubtedly this is the most stupid, senseless and unnecessary war of modern times. It is a war not wanted by Germany, I can assure you, but it was forced on us, and the fact that we were so effectually prepared to defend ourselves is now being used as an argument to convince the world that we desired conflict".'

captors that the only person he had seen shot was a priest who, it was alleged, was a spy. A British despatch later in the year also mentioned a spy. He was in civilian clothes and in the German trenches, pointing out the British positions.

On 22 August, in an attempt to halt the German centre, the Third and Fourth French Armies were ordered to advance in the general direction of Neufchâteau in Belgian Luxembourg. A French officer and a German commander left accounts of the day's fighting at Virton.

The sun was scorching, even though it was only 0900 hours, and to the officer the time was passing slowly. His company was sustaining heavy losses because they were hampering the German advance. 'We were surrounded by a heavy cloud which at times completely veiled the battlefield from our eyes.' One soldier 'sprang up, shouted "Vive La France!" at the top of his voice, and fell dead. Among the men lying on the ground, one could no longer distinguish the living from the dead. The first were entirely absorbed by their grim duty, the others lay motionless, having entered eternal rest in the very attitude in which death surprised them.'

Then there were the wounded. 'Sometimes they would stand up bloody and horrible-looking, amidst bursts of gun-fire. They ran aimlessly around, arms stretched out before them, eyes staring at the ground, turning round and round until, hit by fresh bullets, they would stop and fall heavily.'

Some made no noise but others called out: 'heart-rending cries, agonizing appeals and horrible groans were intermingled with the sinister howling of projectiles. Furious contortions told of strong and youthful bodies refusing to give up life...One man was trying to replace his bloody, dangling hand to his shattered wrist. Another ran from the line holding the bowels falling out of his belly and through his tattered clothes. Before long a bullet struck him down.'

They were holding the German attack with no support. 'We had no support from our artillery! And yet, there were guns in our division and in the army corps, besides those destroyed on the road. Where were they? Why didn't they arrive? We were alone...I was wondering, in my anxiety, whether we were going to lose all our men on the spot.'

As the German Army headed south and west, the French Army marched to meet them. A card sent by a soldier in the German *Fourth Army* in Flanders.

Crown Prince William, who was commanding the German *Fifth Army* in the Virton region, experienced the battle from the reports sent back to his headquarters. After the war he recorded what had happened from the German point of view. 'The action was particularly sanguinary at this point. As I subsequently ascertained for myself, it had cost the enemy's infantry and artillery frightful losses, and the same was unfortunately true of ourselves.' He recalled heavy losses, hundreds of dead including several battalion commanders and a General Staff Officer, and that there was a fog in some areas of the advance.

'About 10 a.m. the attack began along the whole front, and as early as 1 p.m. the enemy, fighting desperately, had been thrown back.' The pursuit continued until darkness fell. His father congratulated him on the victory. 'From His Majesty the Emperor arrived the following telegram: "Congratulations on the first victory which, with God's help, you have won so splendidly. I award you Iron Cross, Classes I and II. Convey to your brave troops my thanks, and those of the Fatherland. Well done! I am proud of you. Your affectionate father, Wilhelm".'

So far the fighting had been against the French and Belgians but now the English Army was reported to be in front of them. To Bloem and his grenadiers, this meant men wearing 'short scarlet tunics with small caps set at an angle on their heads, or bearskins with the chin-strap under the lip instead of under the chin.' Further humour was provided by Bismarck's remark about sending the police to arrest the English Army.

Bloem's unit was enjoying a comfortable midday rest and a hot meal, secure in the knowledge that there was no enemy for fifty miles. As they were finishing their meal, two hussars galloped up. Covered in blood they told them that the enemy was holding the line of the canal in front of them. Shortly afterwards they received orders to move out and attack.

His battalion deployed for the attack. As they left the cover of the wood, a volley of bullets whistled past them causing the first casualties; five or six men collapsed. Moving on, Bloem reached some saddled-up horses. A man in what appeared to be a grey-brown golfing suit and flat-topped cloth cap suddenly appeared, took a shot at Bloem and then ran, after Bloem had shot at him but missed.

The British Army often gave men rum. There was no such tradition in the German Army but this did not stop them imbibing whenever they got the chance. Before contin-

The declaration of war by the British Government turned the European war into a World War. Very quickly the British Expeditionary Force was mobilised and sent to France and then to Belgium. Here the arrival of British Lancers is captured by a Paris photographer.

uing their attack, a corporal produced a bottle of champagne that he had liberated. Lieutenant Gräser asked Bloem for a cup, and the two officers, Corporal Knopfe and orderly Blöse drank the bottle. Gräser prophetically said: "Who knows, it may be our last drink!"

After a smoke they continued the attack. As they rose, the English opened fire. He ordered his men down, but they collapsed voluntarily and involuntarily 'as if swept by a scythe.' After each rush, Gräser had kept up 'a commentary of curses and cheery chatter, but now there was a noticeable silence'. Enquiring as to his whereabouts, he received 'a low-voiced reply: "Lieutenant Gräser is dead, sir, just this moment. Shot through the head and heart as he fell".' The champagne had indeed been his last drink.

'From now on matters went from bad to worse. Wherever I looked, right or left, were dead or wounded, quivering in convulsions, groaning terribly, blood oozing from flesh wounds ... We have to go back ... A bad defeat, there could be no gainsaying it; in our first battle we had been badly beaten, and by the English, by the English we had so laughed at a few hours before.'

This 'first battle fought by the British Army against the Germans came about simply because pre-war plans had placed the British Expeditionary Force in the way of the German advance towards Paris. This position had been agreed during pre-war discussions between the British and French Armies'.

'By 22 August the four infantry divisions and one cavalry division of the BEF had disembarked in France and taken up their positions just across the Belgian border, some miles south of Mons, on the extreme left of the Allied line'. While the British were moving into position the German armies were moving en masse towards the west. 'Their plan had placed much strength on their right flank, which was by now streaming through Belgium with the First Army under von Kluck – the largest of their armies – moving on Ath and Mons'.

'The British command quickly became convinced by cavalry reports, together with those by aerial observation, that German troops were closing in on Mons'. At dawn on 22 August 1914, the British Army met the German Army for the first time.

During the day and in the rear of the cavalry screen, the British infantry took up a thin line of roughly entrenched positions along the Mons-Conde canal, following it round the pronounced salient to the north of the town'. As Bloem's experience proved, the Germans were unaware of the presence of the BEF in this area until the skirmishes that day, 'and even then they did not know the British strength.'

When the mist and rain cleared on the morning of 23 August, there followed, at around 0630 hours, exchanges between German cavalry and British infantry outposts, near Obourg, Nimy and Ville Pommeroeul. The British knew that the main blow would fall along the canal.

Before 0900 hours, German heavy guns were in a position on high ground north of the canal, and opened fire on the British positions. German infantry attacks – units of *IX Corps* – began from across the canal and increased in strength across the salient from Obourg to Nimy. *Infanterie-Regiment von Manstein (Schleswigsches) Nr. 84,* made the first attacks on the Nimy positions. Advancing towards the British infantry in dense lines, they provided easy targets and suffered heavy casualties.

The British troops were ordered to put up a stubborn resistance, and succeeded in

English and Scottish troops captured at the start of the Flanders fighting appear to happy to be in captivity.

holding their positions until after 1100 hours. 'A remarkable feat took place at Nimy, where a Private Niemayer jumped into the canal under fire and closed the swing bridge which enabled the first German troops to cross. The brave Niemayer was killed in the act'.

As *III. Corps* came into action, at Jemappes, two miles west of Mons, the attack moved gradually west along the canal. The withdrawal of British troops north of the canal allowed the attacking troops to get within 200 yards of the bridge at Lock 2. Accurate fire from this position halted the advance. Further west, the *Brandenburg Grenadiers* of *5 Division* fought their way through Tertre to be stopped by the maze of wire fences, boggy dikes and the crossfire of the British troops on the canal bank. By noon, fighting was continuous along the canal. Under continuous observed shelling and infantry attacks, the British battalions to the west began to fall back in the early afternoon. Following hard on the heels of the retreating British troops, the attacking force managed to get over the two unexploded bridges near Frameries.

Shortly after noon, the attacking troops succeeded in passing the canal west of Obourg, and reached the village railway station. Having learned from their recent heavy losses, they had abandoned massed formation attacks, instead deploying in extended order. The situation of the British troops was now precarious: under observation from the heights to the north of the canal, and with German patrols pushing through Mons to their rear, both of the defending battalions began to withdraw by 1515 hours.

This was preceded by a British withdrawal from Nimy where, with only one bridge blown, the defending troops who had stayed were engulfed as the attackers swarmed across the salient, through Nimy and along the straight road into the city.

Fortunately for the British, the attackers did not exploit their success in the canal salient as dusk fell. 'Instead, their buglers were heard to sound the 'cease fire'. However, information arrived from the French 5th Army HQ during the night that Tournai had fallen, and long columns of the enemy had broken through. And a wide gap had opened up on the right between the BEF and Lanrezac's Army. Sir John French had little option but to order a general withdrawal, in the direction of Cambrai, and to try to re-establish contact with his allies'.

An English cemetery in Flanders, looked after by German troops. It is nowhere near as elaborate as an equivalent German cemetery.

The official German account is frank and admits that losses were high: 'Well entrenched and completely hidden, the enemy opened a murderous fire...the casualties increased...the rushes became shorter, and finally the whole advance stopped...with bloody losses, the attack gradually came to an end.'

Bloem's regiment failed to get over the canal and suffered heavily in its failure. Having laughed at the English before the action, the joke was now on them. Their casualties amounted to twenty five officers and far more than 500 NCOs and men. It was his division whose singing was heard that night: 'to cheer themselves, the men sang "Deutschland über alles".'

No matter how hard the French, British and Belgians fought, the German army kept moving forward. On 24 August, 'one million Germans invaded France. For the French and British the great retreat had begun. It lasted for thirteen days, blazing summer days' in which the German Army made a bid for a swift decisive victory. Five of the seven armies 'scythed down towards Paris on a 75-mile front. For the troops on both sides they were days of endless marching under a scorching sun.'

While the battle raged, further units were mobilised and sent to join the invasion. Among them was Herbert Sulzbach, a wartime volunteer, in *63 Artillery Battalion*. He left Aachen on 3 September and within hours saw a trainload of prisoners on their way into captivity. His train's destination was Brussels and, on the way, he noted the ruined villages from the August fighting. 'After a day travelling, the mood changes and it is no longer peaceful; everywhere there are sentries guarding railway crossings and bridges.'

The mood became more tense when later they were told to stop looking out of the train and shut the doors. After two days on the train they reached a temporary halt – Namur. The town was full of troops, passing through, enjoying the cafés or staying on to garrison the city. Although captured only a few days previously, it was now a city under occupation; a city with houses in ruins, with sad-faced inhabitants, a city under curfew. All private houses had to be shut up by 9pm. The war had arrived and was staying; but the main battle front was now in France, where, like Belgium, there were concerns over franc-tireurs.

The Great War.
Ruins round the Town Hall, Louvain.

An example of the damage caused in Louvain. The city fell to the German *First Army* on 19 August 1914 and was relatively peaceful for six days until 25 August when German units to the rear of the city were attacked by a Belgian force advancing from Antwerp.

In a panic and under fire they withdrew to Louvain causing confusion to German soldiers stationed in the city. Shots were heard and troops cried that the Allies were launching a major attack. There was no attack and the authorities blamed the shooting on franc-tireurs. In revenge the city was burnt and looted for five consecutive days. 'Its library of ancient manuscripts was burnt and destroyed, as was Louvain's university (along with many other public buildings). The church of St. Pierre was similarly badly damaged by fire. Citizenry of Louvain were subject to mass shootings, regardless of age or gender.'

Under constant pressure, the ordered and controlled Entente retreat moved closer to Paris, so close that the French government left for Bordeaux on 2 September. But the German Army's fortunes changed when a map was captured that showed that Kluck's *First Army* had changed direction and was heading for the gap between the French Fifth and Sixth armies and not Paris as per the original plan. This exposed his army's right flank to attack at a time when his troops were badly exhausted and seriously over-extended. Exposed on

While some franc-tireurs were shot when they were captured, others were tried by a Field Tribunal consisting of a number of officers.

An aerial view of Termonde, another town destroyed during the German advance.

their rear and flanks, the result was a general withdrawal from the Marne to the Aisne.

From the Aisne the battle moved westwards with each side trying to turn their opponent's open flank and neither securing a strategic advantage. Units leap-frogged each other and on both sides lines of communication were strained in their efforts to move large bodies of men north faster than the enemy. The Western Front moved north from Noyon on 15 September and by 23/24 September was west of Péronne on the Somme. By 27/28 September it was at Bapaume, three days later at Lens and by 8 October was extended by the cavalry of both sides to the region of Bailleul-Hazebrouck.

While both sides raced across the Somme to the Douai Plain, on the night of 19/20 September the British landed a force of marines at Dunkirk who joined the aircraft and armoured car detachment that had stayed in Flanders after their withdrawal from Ostend nearly three weeks earlier. Its aim was to assist the Belgian defenders of Antwerp; a move foreseen by Moltke who had warned General von Beseler, the commanding officer of the troops investing Antwerp, 'that there were signs that the Allies would attempt to raise the siege and attack' communications.

'Simultaneously, on the Western Front, Antwerp was pummelled by the giant

Fort Ertbrand at Antwerp. The gun in the foreground was blown from another position by the artillery barrage.

Map showing German troop movements between August and September 1914.

howitzers that bombarded Namur and Liège. The French along the Aisne under General Edouard de Curière de Castelnau faced mounting pressure from renewed German assaults, and the progress of each corps of the BEF into Flanders was hampered by an

The ruins of Fort Wavre Ste. Catherine after the siege.

Building a replacement bridge over a canal using locally felled timber.

increasingly strong German presence. De Castelnau held on and the BEF pressed on to Ypres so that each corps managed to arrive in the Ypres area just in time to meet the new German onslaught.'

The Antwerp fortress was being invested only from one side, allowing the Belgians to

Map showing the fortress ring at Antwerp.

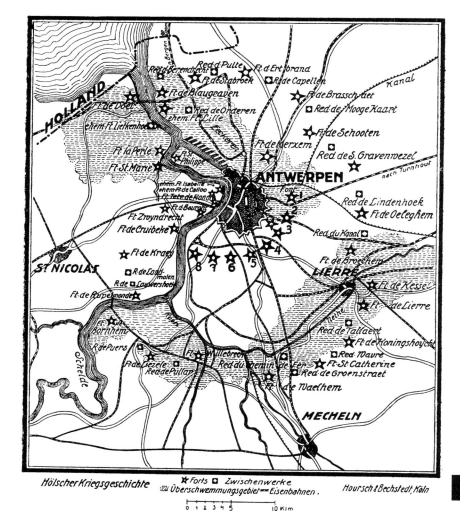

Hölscher Kriegsgeschichte ★ Forts ☐ Zwischenwerke Hoursch & Bechstedt, Köln
☷ Überschwemmungsgebiet ══ Eisenbahnen.

0 1 2 3 4 5   10 Kim

maintain a communication corridor with France. This was now threatened by the movement northwards of both sides and the release of super-heavy artillery after the fall of Maubege. While a general attack on Antwerp was being planned, 5 Division, the Cavalry Division and parts of 4 Division of the Belgian Army advanced against troops moving from Alost. Initially successful on 27 September, *37 Landwehr Brigade,* supported by heavy artillery, reacted so strongly against the attack that the Belgians brought the operation to an end.

The passive investment of Antwerp came to an end the next day with a bombardment of the outer line forts in sector three of the defence line. This was to be followed by an infantry attack from the south.

Drawing troops from garrisons nearby to cover their flanks and with three full divisions available, siege artillery was deployed east and south of Mechelen below Antwerp. The super-heavy guns concentrated on two forts, Wavre Ste. Catherine and Waelham, while heavy guns fired on field defences between the forts and eight-inch mortars targeted two redoubts north-east of Ste. Catherine.

By 1800 hours on 29 September, after just one day's shelling, Fort Wavre Ste. Catherine was so badly damaged that it was evacuated. As Belgian field artillery did not have sufficient range, it was a simple matter for observation balloons to observe every shell landing on the Belgian positions and send corrections when necessary.

The same day, the Belgian Prime Minister told the British minister in Belgium that, if the outer forts fell and an attack was imminent on the second line, then the court, government and 65,000 troops would depart for Ostend, leaving 8,000 men to defend the city. Over the next few days every man who could be spared was transported, along with ammunition and other supplies, out of Antwerp.

The capture of Antwerp would be a feather in von Beseler's cap and a catastrophe for the Entente. At 1600 hours on 1 October, the order was received to assault Forts Wavre Ste. Catherine and Waelhem and the Boschbeek and Dorpveld Redoubts, using *5 Reserve Division* and the *Marine Division.*

By midnight Fort Wavre and Dorpveld had been captured, but Fort Waelhem and

Satirical death notice to the robber band, the Triple Entente and their step sister Belgium, on the fall of Antwerp and its removal from the map by 42cm mortars and motor batteries by the brothers' union of Germany and Austria.

Boschbeek held out until the afternoon of 2 October, 'after all available guns had been turned on to them.' 'During the course of the day (2 October), in consequence of the destruction of gun emplacements, explosion of the magazines and exhaustion of the means of defence, the remaining works in the 3rd Sector, except for Duffel Redoubt, were evacuated or surrendered, and the forts Waelhem and Koningshoyckt were occupied.' The Belgian troops withdrew to new positions.

During 3 October, Duffel Redoubt was evacuated by the Belgians and Fort Kessel shelled by medium guns. The next day, heavy artillery pounded the fort and within a few hours it was out of action and evacuated. On 5 October, two battalions of *26 Reserve Infantry Regiment* crossed the River Nethe, to be joined during the night by two further battalions. With the occupation of Lierre up to the Petite Nethe, the advancing troops had reached the inundation line.

After heavy shelling, Fort Broechem was evacuated on 6 October. However, the Belgian line, although pushed back, was still not broken. A limited Belgian attack succeeded, but because it had no support was driven back, seriously shaken, and as a result pulled further back between the River Nethe and the inner forts. Antwerp's fate was now sealed. In France the battle was moving ever closer to Flanders.

In Artois, *1.Bavarian Reserve Corps* had captured Lens on 5 October and three cavalry corps began a great forward movement on the northern flank. Although *I.* and *II. Cavalry Corps* made no progress, *IV. Cavalry Corps* advancing north of Lille moved in the direction of Ypres and sent patrols over Mont Noir and the Mont des Cats near the Belgian border.

The promised British relief force had not materialised, so during the night of 6/7 October, a number of Belgian divisions pulled back over the Schelde, to join those that had previously departed, leaving a large garrison in the Antwerp defensive ring. As the British tried to organise themselves, *IV. Cavalry Corps*, on the extreme flank of the main army, was approaching Ypres, with orders to get at the left and rear of the main Entente line. As they moved towards Ypres they were unaware of the British force.

Across the Antwerp defensive system the pressure continued. Aided by fog, in the early hours of 7 October, two battalions of *37 Landwehr Brigade* crossed the Schelde in boats and later in the day, after a bridge had been built, the remainder of the brigade crossed. All the Belgian efforts to dislodge them failed. A *Bavarian Cavalry Division,* part of *IV. Cavalry*

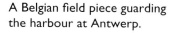
A Belgian field piece guarding the harbour at Antwerp.

Corps, with artillery and infantry was near Ghent, and Fort Broechem was under heavy bombardment. As a result King Albert moved his HQ from to Selzaete and a large part of the Antwerp defence force was ordered behind the Terneuzen Canal.

As the investing force moved forward, it found both Fort Broechem and the Massenhoven Redoubt had been evacuated. The gap in the Antwerp defences was now fourteen miles across. Movement of heavy artillery through this gap allowed the commencement of the shelling of Antwerp using six-inch howitzers, a move hastened by a telegram from OHL that informed General von Beseler that Antwerp needed to be taken soon, as the troops under his command were needed on the right wing of the army.

By the evening, Antwerp's inner forts were defended by the Belgian 2 Division and the British Royal Naval Division. Moving to assist them were a French naval brigade and the British 7 Infantry Division. Opposing them, in the gap between Flanders and the closest Entente positions near Lens, were three cavalry divisions.

Across the Schelde, *37 Landwehr Brigade* was reinforced by *1 Bavarian Landwehr Brigade* and *9 Ersatz Brigade.* The combined force rapidly pushed the Belgian troops back towards the Dutch frontier. Pilots reported the roads from Antwerp were relatively clear but refugees were fleeing towards Holland. The three attacking brigades slowed down the Belgian withdrawal until the night, when the greater part of the Field Army withdrew behind the Ghent-Selzaete Canal. By the night of 8/9 October, the main part of the Belgian Army had escaped.

During 8 October, heavy artillery bombarded forts 3,4, and 5 and the city, while *26 Landwehr Brigade* with some cavalry and a cyclist detachment moved on forts 1 and 2. By 1700 hours these had been abandoned. Shortly afterwards, the defenders started their programme of withdrawal, but a spirited defence of the inner forts deceived the attackers into believing that no retirement was being contemplated.

It was a starlit night and, from their newly captured positions, the investing force could clearly see that Antwerp was on fire. Many houses and barges were burning and oil tanks had been set on fire; a heavy pall of smoke hung over the river. In the morning the inner forts were found to have been abandoned and the bombardment was stopped. A formal

The original German wartime caption for this photo indicated that the reason for the smoke was that the British and Belgian troops had deliberately set fire to the oil depot at Antwerp.

summons to surrender was sent to the Military Governor. At the same time the civilian authorities came out to von Beseler to beg for the cessation of the bombardment. Towards evening, when threatened with a recommencement of the shelling, the fortress capitulated. Only a handful of soldiers were taken the next morning.

As British and Belgians withdrew, they came into contact with the advancing German troops. While many were able to escape, the train carrying a Royal Marine battalion was derailed, and, as the marines tried to continue their journey by foot, part of *1 Bavarian Landwehr Brigade* arrived. In the approaching darkness the battalion extricated itself and moved towards Moerbeke only to bump into a battalion of *1 Landwehr Regiment* that was quickly supported by troops from other nearby units. In all, over 1,300 Belgian and British troops were forced to surrender and became prisoners. Unaware of the general withdrawal from Antwerp, many of the troops broke off contact and turned back in order to trap the non-existent Belgian troops in their fortress.

The troops now released were available to move on the northern flank, taking Zeebrugge and Ostend, but were unable to secure Nieuport and Dunkirk. Neither did they turn the Entente flank. The divisions were now required to cover the approach of four new corps in their advance on Ypres.

The Belgian Army reformed around Ostend, Thourout, Dixmude and Ghent, at the latter together with a French Naval Brigade. A French Territorial division detrained at Poperinghe and the British troops moved from Bruges towards Ghent. When this evacuation was discovered, *III. Reserve Corps,* with *4 Ersatz Division* attached, moved westwards towards Courtrai to extend the front. This was soon changed to the coast at Blankenberghe and Ostend, to be reached by way of Ghent and Bruges.

With the approach of a considerable hostile force, the international force assembled in Ghent withdrew from the city, blowing some of the bridges south of Ghent as they left. Further south the British were advancing in the Hazebrouck area and *IV. Cavalry Corps* had moved away from Ypres, which was then occupied by the French 87 Territorial Division. Further west the Belgians prepared a defensive line on the Yser. As the Entente troops were withdrawing, further to the south British troops at La Bassée and

The inhabitants of Ghent look on as German cyclists arrive to take over the town.

I Marine Division parading through the streets of newly captured Antwerp.

Armentières were attacking the troops who were heading north. The war was now moving into the Ypres area from two directions.

The first troops arrived in Ypres on their way north on 7 October. After requisitioning food for themselves and their horses, the soldiers, cavalrymen, cyclists and infantry were billeted in the town.

The arrival of the German troops was watched by the inhabitants with no apparent concern for the seriousness of the situation. 'Up until then the war had been conducted a long way away from where they lived'. The language barrier allowed little communication but did not stop the troops buying necessities like tobacco and biscuits.

Although originally planning to stay for three days, by midday on 8 October the German troops moved out in the direction of Dickebusch and Vlamertinghe. Nearly a week later, the British arrived. 'The dance of death had reached Flanders.'

As *Sixth Army* had been unable to outflank the French because of the latter's better rail

Political toilet humour comparing the four major cities in Belgium to outside toilets with the German Army in possession and the Allies needing to use the facilities.

Horses and vehicles boarding one of the pontoon ferries. The vessels anchored in the distance were used as pontoons for the bridge which the Anglo-Belgian Army threw across for its retreat. When the last man had crossed the bridge was blown up.

communication, Falkenhayn 'returned to the idea of building a strong strike force on the extreme right wing.' He acknowledged 'that this would be the final throw of the dice for 1914' and emphasised that a breakthrough in Flanders, and against the British in particular, would not only threaten their continued will to resist, but also physically cut them off from the Channel ports and therefore any hope of resupply and reinforcement.'

Falkenhayn believed the prize was worth the stake; nearly everything was to be gambled by both sides on its outcome. He believed it was necessary to eliminate the Allied threat to his right wing so that action could be taken 'against England and her sea traffic with U-boats, aircraft and zeppelins.'

The newly rebuilt *Fourth Army* was assigned the task on 10 October. It was 'to advance, without regard for casualties, with its right wing resting on the coast, first on the fortresses of Dunkirk and Calais... then to swing south.' In conjunction with *6 Army*, it was to 'smash the vulnerable left flank of the Entente forces and thereby deal the enemy an "annihilating blow".' Flanders was now to become the main focus of the western front.

To help put the fighting in context, it is helpful to understand something of the topography of the area. 'The streams which run northwards from the hills about Ypres unite for the most part near the town and flow into the Yser canal, which connects the Lys at Comines with the sea at Nieuport.' On both sides of the canal the land is flat and difficult for observation purposes. As a result any rise was of vital importance to both sides. 'The high level of the water necessitates drainage of the meadows, which for this purpose are intersected by deep dykes which have muddy bottoms.' As the area was quite densely populated it was well provided with roads. Few were paved, so with the frequent rains that begin towards the end of October, they rapidly turn into mud tracks rendering them useless for long columns of traffic.

The high water table and rain impacted upon the construction of trenches. While the loamy soil is quite easy to work in, 'it was only on the high ground that trenches could be dug deep enough to give sufficient cover against the enemy's artillery fire; on the flat, low-lying ground they could not in many cases be made more than two feet deep.'

A German officer described his dugout as a desperate defence against nature: 'Candle

Generalfeldmarschall Wilhelm Leopold Colmar Freiherr von der Goltz. Having served as military governor of Belgium, in 1915 he became military aide to the Turkish Sultan. Goltz died on 19 April 1916, in Baghdad.

stubs lit the dripping, rotting sandbagged walls. Floors were foul-smelling, "viscous mush". Sand-filled sacks hung from the ceilings not always successfully kept food from the reach of rats. Men deloused themselves by sizzling lice in the flame of a candle while others not so fortunate blew on their hands, seized rifles, and ascended for sentry duty. Relieved soldiers would stagger in, blinded by the candles, unbuckle and search for food'.

General Karl von Fasbender, commander of *I. Bavarian Reserve Corps,* likened the fighting in Flanders across rich clover, beet and grain fields, to a type of siege warfare predicted nearly twenty years previously. He explained the difficulties that his troops were up against. The 'villages were little more than a mile apart and interconnected by tree-lined roads and rock fences that constituted a natural defensive network. Their French defenders offered only token resistance along the village perimeter, thereafter falling back to defend the old stone homes.' The Bavarians found that newly-developed trench mortars were highly effective at close range for clearing obstacles and opposition.

A lot had happened in French and Belgian Flanders in a short time: 'the Belgian Army escaped to fight alongside Anglo-French forces in Flanders. Thereafter, Ghent, Lille, Bruges, and Ostend fell within a week.' The news so raised the Kaiser's spirits, recorded

Unwounded and walking wounded Belgian POWs being escorted away from the front.

A very rapidly constructed trench in front of Ypres – autumn 1914.

Admiral Georg von Müller in his diary, that he became 'full of lust for battle...from a distance of 1,000 yards.'

On 14 October, the British, using ground reconnaissance, observed that the positions opposite them had been vacated. Meteren and Bailleul were found to be empty, apart from a small number of severely wounded troops with medical officers, and new positions had been created behind the River Lys. That day OHL had issued an order ending partial offensives, instructing *Sixth Army* to remain entirely on the defensive on a line from La Bassée through Armentières to Menin. The offensive was to be taken up by *Fourth Army* which was to be brought up between Menin and Ypres. The defensive line between Switzerland and the North Sea was solidifying, denying either side the chance to outflank one another, except in Flanders. A siege war with its own routine now set in: 'Eating and sleeping, standing guard, and, in between, trench digging.'

Hundreds of kilometres of trenches had been dug by the end of the year but these would not be enough, even with wire. Experience would show that a further defensive line would be needed, and heavily contested areas would require more. This could not be achieved immediately but when complete this solid line of 'defence in the west would allow attack in the East, and ultimately that assault would be successful.' In the homeland 'the bastion of the Western Front' was known as *Die Gottesmauer* – God's wall.

General Fasbender's *Bavarian Reserve Corps* had taken heavy casualties. 'Battalions shrank to company strength, often led by sergeants-major because their officers had been killed.' French flyers constantly harassed his troops, 'dropping shrapnel bombs loaded with "thick knife blades and sharp hooks" that ripped limbs from bodies.'

Writing from the Great Headquarters on 14 October, the Kaiser welcomed the newly formed *Fourth Army* on its arrival in Belgium. 'I offer my welcome to the *Fourth Army*, and especially to its newly-formed *Reserve Corps*, and I am confident that these troops will act with the same devotion and bravery as the rest of the German Army.

Advance, with the help of God – my watchword.'

Karl Aldag, a twenty-five year old philosophy student, joined his regiment in Belgium on the same day the Kaiser welcomed *Fourth Army*. His company relieved the Bavarian troops who had taken the village. The positions they occupied were far advanced,

A colour-tinted photo of troops crossing the Belgian border at the start of the war.

Nordwestlicher Kriegsschauplatz

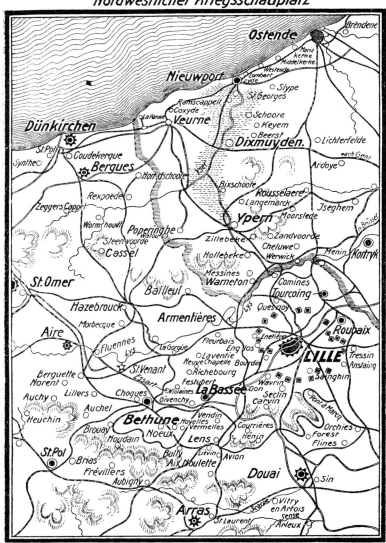

Map of Belgium and northern France.

unfortified and very dangerous. Writing nearly a month later, he described his baptism of fire. 'The fun began on the first day about noon, when shells and volleys of infantry-fire simply poured into the village. We took refuge in the cellars, but as the attack came nearer, we had to go out to defend the place. We had no trenches or any other kind of cover and were fully exposed to shell-fire the whole afternoon. Those were difficult hours, full of fear and horror.' After a brief respite it started up again, to die down finally about 2130 hours. The beautiful starlit night was in complete contrast to the fading battle.

The attack by *Fourth Army* was to be decisive and, on 15 October, the commander, Duke Albert of Württemburg, wrote to the troops to remind them of their responsibility. 'I am pleased to take over the command of the Army entrusted to me by the Emperor. I am fully confident that the Corps which have been called upon to bring about the final decision in this theatre of war will do their duty to their last breath with the old German spirit of courage and trust, and that every officer and every man is ready to give his last drop of blood for the just and sacred cause of our Fatherland. With God's assistance victory will then crown our efforts.

Up and at the enemy. Hurrah for the Emperor.'

Before the main battle commenced, on 16 October, troops in Pervyse picked up a Belgian order that summed up how difficult their attack would be. 'The fate of the whole campaign probably depends on our resistance. I (General Michel) implore officers and men, notwithstanding what efforts they may be called upon to make, to do even more than their mere duty. The salvation of the country and therefore of each individual among us depends on it. Let us then resist to our utmost.'

It was during this period that Crown Prince Rupprecht of Bavaria, exhorting the troops to battle, made clear his feelings for the British and their role in the war. 'When you are fighting this particular enemy (the British) retaliate for his deceit and for having occasioned all this great sacrifice; show him that the Germans are not so easy to wipe out of the world's history as he imagines, show it by redoubling the strength behind your blows. In front of you is the opponent who is the greatest obstacle to peace. On! at him!'

As the line stabilised, both sides pushed at each other's defences during 18 October

A view of the town centre of Menin showing the Hôtel de Ville, the Town Hall.

with considerable activity on both sides. The intention of both was to instigate an offensive that would clear the way for a general advance in the area. While the Entente planned, *III. Reserve Corps* began the battle of the Yser by attacking Belgian outposts east of the river between Dixmude and the sea. The plan was to pierce the Belgian front, wheel south-west, outflank and roll up the Allied line, and at the same time secure the ports. Possession of the coast would obstruct Channel traffic and turn the French flank.

It was a determined attack: 'the men knew they were on the decisive wing of the attack, and they pushed ahead everywhere regardless of loss.' They captured the advanced posts of Keyem and Schoore, and part of Mannekensvere, but were not able to cross the river. The defending Belgians were assisted by the guns of a British flotilla, supported by French units that shelled the advancing troops along the coast as far as Middelkerke. Their effect was more moral than physical as the naval shells exploded into a few large fragments. However, on account of the heavy shelling, *4 Ersatz Division* did not attempt to cross the Yser.

Further south, Allied intelligence discovered that large new formations had detrained southwest of Brussels and were moving towards Ypres. By 17 October their advance guard was at Courtrai and Aerseele. This movement was as a result of a decision taken towards the end of the Antwerp siege.

With the imminent fall of the city and intelligence about Allied concentrations between Lille and Dunkirk, the creation of a new army was ordered. The *Fourth Army,* under the Duke of Württemberg, was to be composed of four recently organised reserve corps, *XXII, XXIII, XXVI* and *XXVII.* The purpose of this army was quite simple – to win the war 'by successfully closing with the enemy, who was still engaged in the concentration and reorganisation of his forces, and by gaining Calais, the aim and object of the 1914 campaign.' Together with *III. Reserve Corps* on its right, it would 'make a decisive breakthrough against the Allied left flank from Menin to the sea.'

The arrival of the new corps was to be covered by the three divisions of *III. Reserve Corps,* who would move north and attack the Belgians when the corps were in position.

A mixed bag of English and Scottish POWs taken during the first Ypres' battles.

Reloading a field gun somewhere in Flanders.

Then *Fourth* and *Sixth Army* would attack across a front from La Bassée to the sea. The phased overlapping attacks would last until the end of November: the Battle of Lille from 15 to 28 October (La Bassée to Messines); the Battle of the Yser, 18 to 30 October (Gheluvelt to the sea); the Battle of Ypres, between 30 October and 24 November (the River Lys to Polygon Wood).

The opinion of the press was that the mercenary English soldier would quickly capitulate and the coming battle for Ypres would be a certain German victory. Even though many of the attacking force were only half-fit, under-trained and untried, they felt confident of success. One officer-correspondent in action near Ypres wrote: 'Eager for the fight and certain of easy victory, the young men of the regiment marched off "to catch the English"…Everyone was firmly convinced that God had given the English long legs so that they could run all the faster…[All] we faced was an army of mercenaries [fighting not] for love of Fatherland or sacrificial courage, but for a few pence a day.'

During 19 October there was 'more or less heavy fighting on the whole front of the *Fourth Army.*' Early in the morning *III. Reserve* and *XXII. Reserve Corps* attacked the Belgian advanced posts on the east of the Yser and shelled Nieuport with heavy guns brought from Antwerp. On *XXIII. Reserve Corps'* front, *45 Reserve Division* reached Handzaeme, six miles east of Dixmude and *46 Reserve Division* reached Staden. Further south, *51 Reserve Division* of *XXVI. Reserve Corps* captured Roulers from the French and *52 Reserve Division* 'drove back the British 3rd Cavalry Division.' During the day an advance of six to nine miles was made by *Fourth Army.*

Private Aldag was one of the troops involved in the fighting on 19 October. 'They attacked. Artillery-fire from three sides. The infantry got so near that we could hear their words of command. Then suddenly our guns started, and that stopped them. Then a merry firing began; they suffered heavy losses, and soon all was quiet. If they had been a little bolder we should all have been done for that day.' Fortunately for Aldag and his comrades the French didn't attack again, contenting themselves with shelling their positions. Being near the coast they were also shelled by the Royal Navy.

Whilst there was considerable fighting on 19 October, the first day of serious fighting was 20 October when both *Fourth* and *Sixth Armies* attacked with the intention of enveloping the British. Opposite Ypres it was 'a hard and bitter struggle for every yard

Heroes' graves in the dunes on the Belgian coast.

of ground' while on *Sixth Army* front, despite fresh reinforcements, a breakthrough was not possible, although some progress was made. The next day the attack by *XXVI.* and *XXVII. Reserve Corps* was held up by strongly entrenched positions on the line Langemarck-Zonnebeke-Gheluvelt. However, on *XXIII. Reserve Corps'* front there was some success. *46 Reserve Division* advanced through Houthulst Forest, with assistance from *45 Reserve Division* to the north, driving 'the French and Belgian cavalry before them.' Further west, *43* and *44 Reserve Divisions* closed in around Dixmude.

Herbert Weisser recorded his experiences during this period: 'during an attack from our side, I was close behind the trench, mending the telephone-wire, under gun- and rifle-fire, with two others. We were without any means of communicating with our troops, and did not know how the battle was going and whether we might not at any moment be cut off by the French. Unarmed! And when, in a hail of bullets, one has to climb up into a tree instead of hiding underground, then one feels that one is young, laughs a little in one's sleeve, and almost fancies oneself invulnerable!'

One of the soldiers killed in the fighting of 20 October was Emil Alefield, a technical student in Munich. On his way to the front, while in Strasbourg, he had written home expressing his desire to fight and if need be die for his country. 'A lot of men I know are off too by the next transport. We are looking forward to it. God will protect us.' He felt he was fighting for a cause: 'we are fighting for our country and are shedding our blood in the hope that the survivors may be worthy of our sacrifice', with the aim of producing 'a pure, true, honourable Germany, free from wickedness and deceit. I will fight and perhaps die for my belief.'

Soldiers quickly became used to death, and to the thought of their own and that of the men around them. Many were more concerned for people at home. Private Weisser wrote to a friend after hearing about the death of a comrade: 'Everybody who goes to the front is prepared for a lonely death…death is no longer horrible when it comes close to one. The only thing that makes it hard to die is the knowledge that one's relations are tormenting themselves by imagining the most ghastly situations…what is there so very dreadful in lying alone on the field of battle and knowing that the end is near? It is not dreadful at all. One can feel calm and peaceful as one has never been since childhood'.

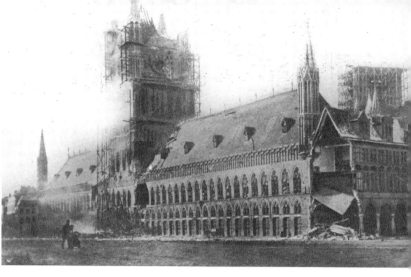

The first damage to the Cloth Hall (Lakenhalle) in Ypres and the Belfry occurred on 5 November 1914 when it was slightly damaged by two German artillery shells. On 21 November an artillery shell hit the Nieuwerck and some of the gable collapsed. On 22 November the Lakenhalle was set on fire by an incendiary device when the scaffolding on the belfry caught fire during an artillery barrage resulting in major damage to the building.

Two of the certainties of war are death and rumour. Hearing the latest rumours, Aldag put them in a letter to his family: 'Dixmude has fallen; America has declared war on England; 1,000 French have deserted; English convicts are being set upon them; many British soldiers carry knives with a special twist in them to scoop out wounded soldier's eyes. Hopes sprang with the news of the right wing going victoriously forward'. While they waited to start their march on Paris, the thunder of the guns never ceased.

In *Sixth Army* sector, the three corps attacked with more vigour than *Fourth Army* but achieved only small local successes. However, this extension of the offensive as far south as La Bassée 'added very considerably to the gravity of the Allied situation, and prevented the withdrawal of troops for use on other portions of the front.'

Even though it had been a day of only limited achievements, men had died achieving these. Herbert Sulzbach, a war volunteer artilleryman, arrived in the Ypres sector on 21 October. His unit, *77 Field Artillery Regiment,* had left Lille only the day before. His first glimpse of the battlefield revealed 'corpses, corpses and more corpses, rubble and the remains of a village.' The British trench he saw was full of dead bodies.

The *Cavalry Corps* were constantly moved around the battle area. Such mass movement was a severe problem; constant entrenching with limited equipment, and the billeting of the numerous horses belonging to eight cavalry divisions, following rainy days and cold nights of travel, produced difficulties well-nigh beyond belief. And, of course, in addition, there was always the enemy to contend with.

Lieutenant Colonel von Baumbach of *8 Jaeger Horse Regiment* recorded how his men fared on 21 October, a day similar to many others. 'Evening found us along the hedges fringing the road to Ypres, proud, glad but hungry, and, though rather tired, we were compelled to dig ourselves in during half the night. We had no spades. Side-arms, pocket knives and hands were requisitioned to scrape, dig, cut and tear off the clods of turf to form the ramparts behind which the men might hide'. So close were they to the English lines that they could hear them digging in with spades. Shooting in the direction of the English lines seemed to keep the area calm; as darkness set, and in order to conserve ammunition, the shooting died down.

The evening was calm and misty, providing some cover for movement. They waited patiently for the scheduled arrival, at 2300 hours, of their meal for the day. 'Bean soup

With few real images of the war available at the start, postcard publishers produced their own interpretations of the conflict. Here German troops are pushing back a mixed group of French and Scottish troops on the Pilckem to Ypres road. The card was sent by a soldier in *46 Reserve Infantry Division*, a unit that had fought in Belgium from the beginning of the war.

was expected to reach us by wagon from Gheluvelt'. However, luck was not on their side. 'It seemed, however, as if the Englishmen had either scented the soup or heard the rattling of the wagon transporting it, perhaps even sensed the hungry unrest prevailing amongst ourselves, for just at the wrong moment – for us – they started a heavy firing from their dugouts. Even the artillery loosened up and rockets ascended, making a hellish noise. Our soup horses came across the fields but the huge kettle was spilled from the wagon, where it was found the next morning. We remained hungry, cold and wet. It was good that we were tired and could sleep at least a little during the night, and did so probably more than we really should have. We blamed the English for all our ills. Next morning brought us recompense in that the English failed to disturb our breakfast.'

After only limited artillery during the night, the offensive continued the next day. Early in the morning of 22 October, two and a half battalions of *III. Reserve Corps* secured a footing on the western bank of the Yser near Keyem and Schoore north of Dixmude. Two principal attacks were made against the British around Ypres: *XXVII. Reserve Corps*

1914 .. Artillerie Anglaise mettant
en position un de leurs gros canons | 1914... British artillery getting in position
one of their big guns (E.L.D.)

The British Army first went into action in Belgium towards the end of August. Following behind the cavalry and infantry were the artillery. Here, assisted by the French they are setting up their gun.

An artillery column riding through Belgium celebrating their success.

attacked from the south-east against Zandvoorde, Becelaere and Zonnebeke; to the north and east the greater part of *XXVI. Reserve Corps,* assisted by a division of *XXIII. Reserve Corps,* attacked Langemarck.

At Langemarck, an attack became a legend: Kindermord (child murder). This is the name given to an assault made by untrained youthful volunteers, many of whom had previously escaped military service. According to reports at the time, the composition of the division was seventy-five per cent kriegsfreiwillige – war volunteers. A more accurate recent analysis shows that the seventy-five per cent were volunteers or untrained, under-aged and over-aged men, the remainder being trained reservists from the Landwehr, Ersatz reserve and Landsturm. These were men who General von Lowenfeld felt were not yet ready for action because their officers lacked tactical knowledge and the men themselves were too prone to manoeuvre in mass.

The British had successfully checked the German attack at Langemarck. At the same time a French offensive against German positions in the Becelaere-Zonnebeke-Passchendaele sector was repelled.

One soldier who witnessed the attacks of the student volunteers was Herbert Weisser, himself a student of architecture at the Technical High School in Charlottenburg. 'Yesterday I was in the trenches. There I have at last been able to see what war is really like. The whole business is enacted on one narrow, though certainly endless, strip of ground, which seems much, much too narrow for its gigantic significance. And this strip of ground bears grass, many coloured flowers, trees, and pretty little houses. The ground rises and falls gently, the green fields are intersected by hedges and streams. But do you know what else is in these meadows? The Marburg Jaegers, students and professors, the hopes and impetus towards progress of the German people. One beside the other they lie, stretched out upon the grass'.

Musketier Scheidhauer described how hard the day had been: 'Never again did I experience so tough an assault as this one. Whistles blew to signal the start. A warrant officer was lying to my front. "Herr Feldwebel, we must get going!" I pulled at his foot, but he lay there stiffly. He was dead. At the end of the next bound an Unteroffizier was lying down on the ground. I pulled at his clay covered boot. Stiff – dead. I shuddered all over.'

As the attackers closed in, there were numerous vicious fights at close range with fixed bayonets. 'Frequently they advanced against volley fire at ranges of less than fifty metres with inevitable consequences for the advancing troops. Perhaps due to their inexperience, the attackers pressed home their assaults long after there was any real hope of achieving a breakthrough'. Losses were heavy. By the end of the day, the three battalions of *Reserve Infantry Regiment 215* had been reduced to four weak composite companies; nearly every officer had become a casualty.

Although the attack had fallen well short of expectations, there were minor successes. 'A party, comprising men of *Reserve Jäger Battalion 18* and elements of *Reserve Infantry Regiment 213,* …launched a successful attack on Bikschote mill, capturing 150 British soldiers in the process.'

As darkness fell and the artillery shelling dropped, close to the British lines there was a great moan. In the glow of a burning farmhouse the casualties of the attack could be heard and seen. A British officer reported that he could see men 'with their arms and legs off trying to crawl away; others who could not move gasping out their last moments with the cold night wind biting into their broken bodies.'

The next day a limited British attack against Cabaret was successful; as a result, fifty-four Scottish POWs who had been captured previously were released, and the British claimed to have captured 350 men of *45 Reserve Division*. During the morning, British positions were shelled and, at around 0800 hours, a strong force moved from Koekuit, covered by very heavy artillery fire, against British positions near Langemarck. Against determined resistance, the attackers started to withdraw around 1300 hours. Similarly, a French attack during the afternoon was unsuccessful.

The official account admits that the two days did not achieve as much as had been hoped. 'With the failure of the *46th Reserve Division* to gain a decisive victory between Bixschoote and Langemarck on the 22nd and 23rd October, the fate of the *XXVI.* and *XXVIII. Reserve Corps* was also settled. For the time being, any further thought of a breakthrough was out of the question.'

The Bavarian General von Fasbender described the situation the troops faced and fought in, commenting especially on the villages where the conditions and the fighting

To war with music, flowers and the company of their families; troops march to the railway station ready to leave for the front.

General von Falkenhayn was commander in chief of the German Army until August 1916. 'Falkenhayn succeeded Moltke as Chief of the General Staff of the German Army after the Battle of the Marne on 14 September 1914. Confronted with the failure of the Schlieffen Plan due to Moltke's interference, he attempted to outflank the British and French in the "Race to the Sea", a series of engagements throughout northern France and Belgium in which each side tried to turn the other's flank until they reached the coastline.' The card was sent by a soldier in *2 Labour Company of 1 Bavarian Infantry Division* to his friend serving in *SMS Ostfriesland*, the second vessel of the Helgoland class of battleships

were terrible. 'We have to conquer the houses one by one, drag the enemy out of the cellars and storage sheds, or kill them by throwing hand-grenades down at them. The casualties are always high… All churches, including their steeples, are destroyed, all roofs torn off, walls caved in, entire houses bared to the elements; human beings and animals lie about, the barns are empty, cows roam about lowing, horses stand stupidly in the middle of roads; none are fed, watered, or milked because no one has remained in the villages.'

In a letter home, Infanterist Ernst Topper, serving with *121 Infantry Regiment*, after writing that he thought 'Mankind is an animal of the vilest sort', reported the same scenes as had General von Fasbender: 'Horses, hogs, cows have in some cases been burned, or shriek; where left tied-up (they stand) and shriek mercilessly out of hunger and thirst.'

Paul Rohweder, a student of theology at Kiel, who was killed near Het Sas on 23.4.15, wrote home to explain his surroundings: 'Under a golden poplar lies a dead comrade. In the peasants' farmyards lie dead cattle. The windows are broken by shell-fire. Not a bird is to be seen. All nature holds its breath with fear'.

Fasbender also noted that morale was plummeting among the German troops due to general exhaustion. However, the same was not true on the French side of the battle-field. Sensing that the troops facing them were mostly newly-raised units, and deciding that these would be unlikely to sustain a strong defence, an attack was ordered the next day. Attack was followed by counter-attack and, with the arrival of reinforcements, the French and British were able to finish the day on new positions between 500 and 1,000 yards further east, and with the capture of Zonnebeke.

Time was running out for the offensive. 'On 23 October Falkenhayn told Albrecht and Rupprecht that their conduct of operations would be reviewed unless more success was forthcoming, the gains at such cost having been purely tactical'. Rupprecht's chief of staff

Reserve-Infanterie-Regiment Nr. 243.

Uns treibt nicht Eroberungslust, uns beseelt der unbeugsame Wille, den Platz zu bewahren, auf den Gott uns gestellt.

4. August 1914   Wilhelm II.

Regimental pride is clearly displayed in this card. *243 Reserve Infantry Regiment* had fought in Belgium since the start of the war, suffering heavy casualties during First Ypres. The card was sent by a soldier in the regiment's second battalion to his wife in Adorf a month before his division moved to the Champagne to fight against the French.

proposed a reduction in the *Sixth Army* frontage, while Albrecht wanted the offensive to move away from Ypres against French and Belgian positions in the north. These attacks were to start the next day.

Although exhausted, troops from *XXVII. Reserve Corps* continued the battle, with unsuccessful attacks during 23 and 24 October on Polygon Wood and on Gheluvelt crossroads. In one unsuccessful attack on British positions at Kruiseecke, 200 men of *242 Reserve Infantry Regiment – 54 (Württemberg) Reserve Division –* were taken prisoner (many of those captured during this period were rated by their captors as young, unfit and lacking in morale). Positions in the French and Belgian sectors were assaulted with the support of super-heavy artillery fifteen times over a five hour period, but each time the attack was repulsed. South of Nieuport, an attack by *5* and *6 Reserve Divisions* with five supporting battalions from *44 Reserve Division* succeeded in crossing the Yser but were unable to transport any artillery over with them.

Inadequate rations meant men were eating raw turnips from the fields and risking shell fire to collect them. Even in their trenches there was little protection. 'Casualties continued to mount as they clung on in unsuitable, inadequate, badly located trenches, which had simply been dug as a reflection of where the ebb and flow of the battle had come to a halt.'

Captured letters showed the effect of British artillery fire on the troops of *XXVII. Reserve Corps*. A soldier from *246 Reserve Regiment* wrote: 'on the 24th October we were ordered to be ready for an assault before dawn. We had hardly advanced five hundred yards when we were met by a terrible shell fire from the English. When we were collected again I found what an awful disaster had overtaken us. Of our battalion scarcely eighty men came through.'

The accuracy of the shelling was attested to by a soldier in *242 Reserve Regiment:* 'The shooting of the English artillery is marvellous. They get the right range and direction every shot, and place each shell within a yard of the previous one. They must be wonderfully well informed of our movements. I don't know whether the intelligence is obtained by their aeroplanes, which are always hovering over us, or whether they have telephones behind our lines.'

The ruins of Langemark after the fighting had moved on and there had been time to clear the roads.

'The situation around Langemarck on 24 October was one of totally confused chaos and the entire battlefield was littered with dead and dying soldiers.' By nightfall on 24/25 October the fighting was over and the reserve corps involved, owing to a lack of company officers and heavy losses, were practically incapable of further offensive action. Acknowledging this, Duke Albrecht, commanding *Fourth Army*, ordered *XXIII., XXVI.* and *XXVII. Reserve Corps* 'to maintain and strengthen their positions, and to take every opportunity of seizing important points on their immediate front.' In the north, the road to Calais and Dunkirk appeared potentially to be open, as the defending Belgian and French troops were exhausted. Duke Albrecht therefore directed that the attacks be continued in that area.

Sunday 25 October was a gloriously sunny day and Private Kurt Peterson was glad to greet it after his recent baptism of fire. He was in the trenches near Dixmude and during a quiet period found time to write a letter to his parents. Peterson was a philosophy student in Berlin when he volunteered at the start of the war. In his letter he described his recent experiences. 'I never thought to see it [the sun] again! Terrible were the days which now lie behind us. Dixmude brought us a baptism of fire such as scarcely any troops on active service can have experienced before: out of 180 men, only 110 unwounded; the 9th and 10th Companies had to be reorganized as one; several Captains killed and wounded; one Major dangerously wounded, the other missing; the Colonel wounded. Our Regiment suffered horribly. It was complemented by the Division'.

Unlike British servicemen's mail, his letter was not censored by his commanding officer so he was able to describe what war felt like. 'What experiences one goes through during such an attack! It makes one years older! Death soars around one; a hail of machine-gun and rifle bullets; every moment one expects to be hit; one is certain of it. One's memory is in perfect working order; one sees and feels quite clearly. One thinks of one's parents. Then there rise in every man thoughts of defiance and of rage and finally a cry for help: away with war! Away with this vile abortion brought forth by human wickedness! Human-beings are slaughtering thousands of other human-beings whom they neither know, nor hate, nor love. Cursed be those who, while not themselves obliged to face the horrors

Bataillons - Stabsquartier in Westflandern in einem von Engländern und Franzosen zusammengeschossenen Hause.

A house in West Flanders destroyed by British and French shelling. Although damaged, it still provided sufficient cover to be used as a battalion headquarters. Three officers and four enlisted men can be seen in the foreground. Another card sent by a soldier in *52 Reserve Division*, this time by a member of the *divisional pioneer company* to his wife.

of war, bring it to pass! May they all be utterly destroyed, for they are brutes and beasts of prey!'

Writing from Vieux Chien to his fiancée on 25 October, war volunteer Paul Hub described his life in Flanders. 'Will there ever be a normal Sunday again? The terrible digging continues. Every day brings new horrors. Yesterday, while trying to dismount our telephone line we ended up in the middle of heavy infantry and grenade fire. We were incredibly lucky to get out unscathed. It's impossible to get rid of these Englishmen…When the enemy finds us, we might be on the move again. I'm slowly getting used to the noise. My hearing has come back again after the effect of shells exploding right next to me yesterday.'

Not all attacks faltered and failed. On 26 October, the bombardment of Kruiseecke was renewed. Heavy artillery shells destroyed the British trenches, burying men in the sandy soil. This was to be followed by a fifteen battalion attack. Before this some of the attackers had got through to a wood behind the British lines from where they called out in English for the troops to retire when the main attack was launched at 1000 hours. This withdrawal allowed the attackers to get behind the advanced British positions and take the defenders prisoner. One senior casualty of the day was General von Meyer, commander of *2 Ersatz Brigade*, who was killed 'in the heat of the fighting' during the evening.

Throughout this period the bravery of the German soldier was noted by their enemies. They 'had attacked with great courage, officers carrying regimental colours ran on ahead of the men and planted the colours in the ground to give their men a point to make for, a mounted officer rode forward, exposing himself recklessly, to encourage his soldiers.' However, time after time the accurate shooting of the British stopped the charge.

To maintain the speedy advance of its army, the German Supreme Command issued orders to confiscate much of the food and supplies from the local population. Living off the land was not always easy as war volunteer Hub told his fiancée. 'Everyone has to find their own food. Sometimes we manage to throw together a decent soup. You can find meat on the farms. We just don't have enough bread. I've got a few pieces of chocolate and other tasty morsels in my rucksack that I got from you and our parents.'

England was seen as the main enemy as can be seen by this card sent by a soldier in training to his wife.

Another problem was the isolation. 'You just don't realise how lonely you get when you're cut off from the rest of the world like this. Now I understand why people were begging for newspapers at all the German-occupied train stations…Please write when you get this. The post here is very slow.'

The weather was rapidly deteriorating and both food and water were in short supply. Wilhelm Brendler of *Reserve Infantry Regiment 233* later recalled his time in the trenches during autumn 1914. For over a day the pouring rain had been 'turning all the bottoms of the trenches into small lakes, puddled by the impermeable clay. The walls began collapsing and we were completely plastered with mud. It clung to our boots, our hands and our faces like glue…It was not so bad if it was possible to hide away in a hole cut into the forward trench wall out of the wind, or if there was some small dry place in which to squat'. Movement was extremely unpleasant: 'great courage had to be mustered to wade through these muddy ponds and lakes where the water was often knee deep.'

It was not possible to keep clean or bury the dead in such conditions. Brendler recalled: 'We had not had a wash in eight days. Corpses, which we had so far not been able to bury, lay all along the Haenixbeek (stream), so there was no question of being able to drink the water, nor was there enough to eat'. The field kitchens could not get up to the front so getting hot food was extremely difficult and dangerous. Many ration parties paid with their lives.

Both the *Fourth* and *Sixth Armies* had failed in their allocated objectives and as a result the *OHL* began to consider a plan for concentrating another army or army group between the two armies already fighting in Flanders with the intention of breaking through south of Ypres. 'On the 27th October, General von Falkenhayn, Chief of the General Staff, arrived at *Sixth Army* headquarters to make the final arrangements and issue orders.'

This was not mentioned to the troops in the daily news sheets, produced by Army and Corps Headquarters, that were pinned up wherever they would be seen by as many troops as possible, to provide war news from all the fronts. Each eagerly read edition gave news about the situation in Russia, on the Somme, or closer to home on the Flanders front. A Corps news sheet for 27 October provides an example of a typical day's news:

A German officer inspects the remains of British dug-outs in Polygon Wood.

'The fighting on the Yser-Ypres Canal front is exceedingly violent. In the north we have succeeded in crossing the canal with a strong force. East of Ypres and south-west of Lille our troops have advanced slowly after severe fighting. Ostend was yesterday bombarded by the English ships.'

That same day, Adolf Hitler's unit received orders to move to Ypres 'where a battle was under way, which newspapers described as a "fight for life and death" for the German people.' At 0200 hours, they marched to the Place de Concert in Lille to listen to an order from their commanding officer, the Bavarian Crown Prince. 'We have now the fortune to have the Englishmen on our front, the troops of that people whose antagonism has been at work for so many years in order to surround us with a ring of enemies and strangle us. We have to thank them above all for this bloody, terrible war…[When] you meet up with this enemy, [show] them that the Germans cannot be swept so lightly from world history…Onwards! Onwards!'

Private Peterson wrote home regularly to keep his parents abreast of his experiences. Two days after his previous letter, he described what happened after the warming October sun had gone down. 'In the night of the 25th, we were overtaken by rain in the trench. I don't know how many nights we have not lain out in the cold and wet without proper food or shelter, and so it has been till today. That same night we came out of the trench towards 2 o'clock. I was attached to the *2nd Company*. Where my own Company is, I don't know. There was an attack on Dixmuide (sic). Ghastly! A repetition of the first attack. Again frustrated by the awful machine-gun fire. The half-uttered 'hurrah' was choked. We all lay like logs on the ground and all about us death hissed and howled. Such a night is enough to make an old man of one.'

Most of the men had gladly gone to war. Now only twelve weeks later the stark reality of war had changed many minds. Private Peterson was not afraid of death and was prepared for it. It would at least be a way to get out the horrors he found himself in. He had survived two attacks and did not want to be in another; all he wanted was to go home. 'We have had enough of war…Away, with this war! Put an end to it as speedily as possible!' However, the same night he wrote the above there was yet another attack.

A decision had been taken to form an army group with General von Fabeck in command. This new formation was created by transferring local divisions and by bringing *II. Bavarian Corps* from the Somme and *XV. Corps* from the Aisne. Also attached were a corps of cavalry, a Landwehr brigade and six unattached battalions. The new army group was also provided with over 250 heavy artillery pieces. 'A general offensive by the right wing and centre of the *Sixth Army, Fabeck's Army Group,* and the whole of the *Fourth Army*

A squad using a ditch for cover as they move through a wood somewhere in Belgium. The card was sent to Fraulein Paula Schieffer by Musketeer Fischer of *2 Battalion 237 Reserve Infantry Regiment in 103 Reserve Brigade of 52 Reserve Division*. This division had served in Belgium since the start of the war and at the time of sending Musketeer Fischer was serving in front of Ypres.

was ordered for the 30th, when Fabeck was to break through.' The build-up of such a force would be obvious.

From midnight on 28/29 October the town of Ypres was bombarded. On the Belgian front the attack on Dixmude slackened due to a lack of ammunition, but north of the town troops of *III. Reserve Corps* and *44 Reserve Division* were able to advance slowly. The Belgian opening of the sluice gates on 27 October effectively halted any progress as the sea rapidly inundated the area, creating a lake nearly a mile wide between the opposing forces.

This inundation was first attempted when the tides were too low but the next night met with greater success. The opening of eight sluice gates began to flood the area between the Yser and the railway embankment. With higher than average tides, the operation was continued over the next three nights and by 28 October the water was between Dixmude and Pervyse, reaching the latter on 31 October. Eventually, a lagoon, between eighteen and twenty-one miles long, between one and three quarters and two and a half miles wide and three to four deep was created.

As the water, originally thought to be temporary flooding caused by heavy rainfall, spread, it impacted on troop positions and eventually rendered any movement impossible. Troops in front of the Belgian positions were already suffering from a shortage of supplies, due to heavy shelling of bridges and roads, before the inundation made the situation worse. The diary of an officer in *202 Reserve Infantry Regiment* recorded the lack of hot food, the inadequacy of the bread ration and the fact that emergency rations were almost exhausted. There was no fresh water; the men resorted to drinking whatever could be found, even if it was green.

Although Private Peterson wanted only to go home, he was not afraid to take risks for his fellow soldiers. He had escaped with his life in the attack, but French fire had stopped him bringing in three wounded comrades who were lying out in the open. They managed to bring one man in but the French showed no sympathy for their attempts to rescue the wounded and redoubled their fire. On his second attempt his helpers deserted him, leaving him with two wounded men. Knowing he could only bring one in, he asked them to decide. The younger of the two pointed to the badly wounded older family man and

French marines conveying an armoured car on a raft across the Yser Canal to escape the advancing Germans.

told Peterson to take him, but begged him to come back for him as soon as possible. On reaching safety, he immediately asked for permission to do this, but was refused. In the evening, the officer gave in and scoured the company for volunteers to accompany Peterson. They returned shortly with the wounded man in a ground-sheet. Just under a year later, brave Private Peterson was killed fighting in Russian Poland.

To cover the concentration of troops, *I. Cavalry Corps, 6 Bavarian Reserve Division* and *XXVII. Reserve Corps* were to attack Gheluvelt on 29 October. This was to be the start of a full-scale attack on the Ypres front. Buoyed up by propaganda that had lulled them into a false sense of complacency, the Bavarians were to suffer heavily both from the enemy and their own side. Hitler's regiment, wearing Landsturm caps, were mistaken for

Password 'Goodbye'. Destination Paris, London, Petersburg. Six older reservists of *17 Reserve Division* pose for a farewell photograph. Taken while they were guarding the Schleswig-Holstein coast, the men were under orders to move out. On 23 August they left for Louvain arriving at the time of the mass destruction of the town.

German troops resting in the ruins of Kemmel.

Englishmen by Württemburg troops who shot and killed a number of them. Inexperienced but full of élan, the Bavarians made a successful initial rush, but as they continued their attack they failed to check the captured trenches. As a result, they were shot at from behind.

Although in this first fight they lost over 300 men, the day was still regarded as a success. Colonel List advised the battalions: 'Enemy thrown out of all his positions, several hundred prisoners. Infantry holds the positions won and is digging in there. Reinforcements from the *6. Res. Inf.-Division* are expected soon.'

The reserve corps had attacked, since their arrival, 'with considerable courage and died in large numbers.' Some of the regiments had certainly lost up to fifty per cent as casualties, while it is possible that some may have lost up to seventy per cent of their effectives. Brave they were, sacrificed, certainly, as they had gone into battle 'with no overview of the strategic situation, no clear knowledge of the terrain, the strength and positions of the enemy, or of the appropriate fighting tactics.' As many of them were untrained, they were 'too helpless, particularly when the officers had been killed.'

On the morning of 30 October, the Allied commanders were still unaware of the massing of reinforcements opposite their tactically weakest and strategically most important sector. The order from General von Fabeck found on the body of an officer of *XV. Corps* provided the Allies with some idea of what was to come. 'The break-through will be of decisive importance. We must and will therefore conquer, settle for ever with the centuries-long struggle, end the war, and strike the decisive blow against our most detested enemy. We will finish with the British, Indians, Canadians, Moroccans, and other trash, feeble adversaries, who surrender in great numbers if they are attacked with vigour.'

The main effort of the offensive was to be made by Fabeck's Army Group against the British south-east of Ypres. Its first objective was 'to be Zandvoorde and Messines Ridge, with the object of breaking through to Kemmel Heights, cutting off all the Allied troops in and north of Ypres,' driving them against the coast or into Holland. In order to draw reserves away from the planned attack, *XXVII. Reserve Corps* would attack an hour earlier against the junction of the British and French troops near Zonnebeke. The attack that

A company ready to move out receiving its orders.

began at 0630 hours on 30 October would in fact not reach fruition for another three and a half years when Kemmel was finally taken from the French.

The diversionary attack started with an artillery bombardment of the British trenches and the area behind them at 0600 hours. Thirty minutes later strong infantry attacks attempted to split the junction between the British and French Armies. By 0900 hours, despite heavy losses, some troops had reached the wire which an officer attempted to cut; the attack then petered out. Weaker attacks were attempted at 1120 and 1200 hours. Again neither succeeded and the official account recorded that 'it had not the success expected' even though two divisional generals, General von Deimling and Major-General Wild von Hohenborn, went in to the front line near Gheluvelt, to encourage the men. The attack resulted in heavy losses and no gain.

Between 0645 and 0800 hours 'fire was poured on the trenches' in front of Zandvoorde and the area directly behind. In narrow trenches that offered little cover, many of the defenders were buried; when *39 Division* and three *Jäger* battalions attacked, the British retirement failed to save the dismounted cavalry on the left flank, who were cut off and annihilated, only a few wounded being taken prisoner. After a cautious advance, Zanvoorde was in the possession of *39 Division* by 1000 hours.

British counter-attacks failed. By mid-afternoon, 'the British were forced back to the edges of the small woods which mark the line from Hollebeke Château to the southern boundary of the grounds of Herenthage Château, about three thousand yards north of Zandvoorde.' The arrival of considerable British reinforcements brought this attack to a standstill.

During the middle of the morning, south of Zanvoorde, *II. Bavarian Corps* attacked with *4 Bavarian Division* to the north and *3 Bavarian Division* south of Comines canal against two British dismounted cavalry divisions. Although the bombardment was quite heavy, the attacking infantry showed little determination except near Hollebeke Château. Similarly, *30 Division* also made no progress.

Towards noon, artillery moved up and *II. Bavarian Corps* troops concentrated on British positions near Hollebeke village. The retirement of the British troops 'brought the Bavarians within three miles of the town of Ypres' and allowed them to close round the château. *II. Bavarian Corps* troops continued to press forward, causing the British to withdraw to their prepared second line across the top of the Ypres Ridge to the canal bridge.

An artillery unit advancing in the rain.

As the Bavarian troops did not press their attack further, the lines stabilised.

The attack near Messines, made by *26 (Württemburg) Division* in the evening, was repulsed even though the British positions had been heavily shelled. However, *122 Fusilier Regiment* took possession of, according to British sources, the unoccupied hamlet of Wambeke, though the regimental history of the regiment states it was occupied by Indian troops under English officers. Similarly, attacks further south by a cavalry corps against St. Yves failed to take the town, and *XIX. Corps* on their left flank also made no progress.

However, some of the attacking troops had made more progress and had got through the British lines in the confusion of battle. Fortunately for the British their number was small; had they been greater in number they could have created much mayhem from their hidden positions in the woods behind the front line. Being few in number, they were able only to harass individuals and small parties as they brought materials to the front, before being captured or returning to their own lines under cover of darkness.

In the north, despite the rising water level caused by the inundation, *III. Reserve* and *XXII. Reserve Corps* attempted to attack the Belgian positions. *5 Reserve Division,* near the coast, although shelled by the Royal Navy, crossed the Dixmude-Nieuport railway embankment, the main Belgian line of defence and took Ramscappelle. On their left flank, *6 Reserve Division* got close to Pervyse but the next two divisions, *43* and *44 Reserve Divisions,* although across the Yser, failed to make any progress.

The possession of Ramscappelle was only brief; it was retaken during the night by a Belgian counter-attack. It was the closing act of the battle of the Yser. Shortly afterwards *5 Reserve Division* began its retirement and *6 Reserve Division* reported that it could no longer attack because of the rising water. 'On the morning of the 30th the advancing troops had been up to their ankles in water; then it had gradually risen until they were' wading up to their knees, scarcely able to drag their feet out of the clayey soil.' The green meadows were now covered in dirty, yellow water.

To save his troops from being cut off by the rising water, General von Beseler ordered the retirement of *III. Reserve Corps* but left *XXII. Reserve Corps* in position across the Yser until 2 November when it too was forced to pull back by rising water levels. According

In most cases both sides treated the dead respectfully. This shows the grave of a solitary French soldier who died in the coastal fighting of 1914 and was buried by his enemies.

to Captain Schwink in the OHL history of the battle 'in spite of the dangers due to the altered appearance of the country and the consequent difficulties in finding the way, and although the Franco-Belgian artillery kept the Yser crossings under constant heavy fire, the withdrawal was a brilliant success. Not a wounded man nor rifle fell into the enemy's hands, and the movement was so well covered that the enemy did not notice we had disengaged until it was too late.'

Not all units were able to disengage themselves as easily as Captain Schwink suggested. A small group of Brandenburgers under Leutnant Bucholz remained in Pervyse after the main withdrawal. With the sea on one side and enemy artillery fire in front of them, the French offered Bucholz honourable conditions if he would surrender. Indignantly rejecting the offer, he slipped off with his troops to successfully rejoin their unit.

While the rising water protected the Allied left flank, the Belgian Army stayed in place. The water also protected the attackers from Allied attack, thereby releasing thousands of troops for service further south at Ypres, where, unaffected by the water levels, the French lost Bixschoote. On 30 October, the German effort on the Yser front effectively ended.

Losses on both sides had been high. The British were receiving few reinforcements and had exhausted their reserves. On the German side, Colonel Bauer wrote that their attacks had 'cost the most dreadful sacrifices in blood, and very little had been achieved.' However the battle would continue 'in spite of protests from divisional commander because Crown Prince Rupprecht had ordered them in very hard words.' It would continue the next day between Messines and the Comines Canal.

The fine weather on 31 October and the clearing of the morning mist allowed the use of observation balloons to direct the fire of heavy artillery onto the British positions – something the British would not be able to copy until late May of the following year.

On 31 October, the Kaiser left Douai to visit the troops, ending his tour at Warneton where he visited General von Schubert, commander of *XIV. Reserve Corps*. Admiral von Müller recorded in his diary that the weather was marvellous and that 'the front line was not more than 3 kilometres away so that rifle and machine gun fire could be heard'. They

Landsturm garrison troops in Louvain. Older troops released younger ones for active service. These quite elderly troops are wearing the Model 1888 Prussian Landwehr Mannschaften Tschako.

saw wounded troops and English prisoners coming down the line before returning to the safety of Douai.

Paul Hub, serving in *247 Reserve Infantry Regiment* – it later became known as 'The Regiment of the Dead' – wrote to his fiancée describing his recent experiences. 'There are lots of Scots amongst all the dead and wounded. Instead of trousers they wear a sort of short, warm skirt that only reaches halfway down their thighs. Well it's not really a skirt, it's more of a sort of folded wrap-around thing. It is a strange sight. I'm amazed the boys don't freeze their bums off, walking around half-naked like that, because they don't wear any underwear either. That said, they do have a warm, heavy coat like the other English soldiers.'

With the initiative in the hands of the attackers, the main effort was made in the southern sector between Messines and the Comines Canal. During the night of 30/31 October, the British positions were constantly sniped and intermittently shelled by 20cm

Shell craters in the road being filled in by engineers.

Religious print on the wall of a destroyed house in Poelkapelle.

howitzers. Around 0400 hours, men of *119 Grenadier* and *125 Infantry Regiment* attacked the trenches defended by Indian troops, between the Douvre river and Messines, cheering and blowing horns. Some of the attackers rushed through to the support line, where those that actually got into the trench were bayoneted or shot, or ran off. As daylight appeared, the attackers pulled back under rifle and artillery fire. Attacks to the north also met with no success.

The next attack was centred on the village of Messines. As the mist lifted, a barrage of heavy artillery and trench mortars was concentrated on the village. An hour later, at 0900 hours, *26 Division* troops began their assault. The numbers and force of the attackers forced the British to pull back to a second position in the village.

The assault on the village continued, assisted by engineers with demolition charges and a field gun. Fighting from house-to-house, the British were forced to pull back until around mid-day when British reinforcements arrived and counter-attacked, recapturing some of their lost trenches and only a few houses and the convent. The fighting continued through the night.

Wytschaete, a much larger village, was also attacked on 31 October. *3 Bavarian Division* of *II. Bavarian Corps* was designated to assault the British positions between Wytschaete and the Comines canal with *6 Bavarian Reserve Division* on its left flank, between it and *26 Division* at Messines.

By the end of the day, no progress had been made, so *6 Bavarian Reserve Division* was held back for a night assault on the town. This was launched at 1645 hours but, after forty-five minutes, petered out. At 2215 hours a further attack was made; this again failed to break through the British positions and was repulsed. Shelling and sniping continued through the night, but no further attack was made.

30 and *54 Divisions* were initially more successful than the other attacking divisions. After heavy fighting, they managed to capture Gheluvelt, a situation that had serious repercussions for the British and the Ypres Salient.

16 Bavarian Reserve Infantry Regiment took part in the assault on Gheluvelt. Along with Fromelles and the Somme battles, it was a celebrated engagement described in detail in the regimental history: 'The losses grow under the violent fire that the enemy hurls towards the attackers from cannon and machine-guns. They lean and fall down on their knees among the hedges, mown down by [the] burst of fire – but the yawning gaps are always filled by fresh fighters. Our artillery's lack of ammunition is clearly noticeable; it can offer the attack no effective support.'

Throughout the morning there were tough, bloody stand-up fights with new waves of men replacing those who fell until 1500 hours when the heavy artillery smashed the wind-

With so many men arriving in Belgium in such a short period of time every available space was used as a bivouac. Here infantry rest in a church.

mill strongpoint. The troops rushed forward: 'A thousand-voiced Hurrah roars across the battlefield, a single violent victory cry – and like a wild surf the storm waves throw themselves at the village! – Gheluvelt is ours!'

The victory was short-lived. Counter-attacks by the British in the château area held, and then forced back, the attackers. Similarly, those troops who had pushed on from the village came under heavy fire and retired to the village. A major British counter-attack later cleared the village and restored the gap in the British line.

'The British counter-offensive took the raw Bavarian troops and their few remaining officers completely by surprise.' When a company of British regulars entered the village they found the Bavarians 'enjoying the repose of victory, searching for water and looting, and in no expectation of such an onslaught. They offered no organised resistance and were soon fleeing back in confusion through the village.'

The *List Regiment* had lost heavily in men and in officers, including its commanding officer Colonel List. In the Bavarian official history, the regiment's participation was described as having being fought under unfavourable circumstances resulting in heavy losses. The official communiqué for 30 October was brief: 'Our attacks to the south of Nieuport and to the east of Ypres were completed successfully. Eight machine-guns were captured along with eight hundred Englishmen.' The report of the fighting on 31 October stated simply: 'The attack on Ypres continues.'

Although Ypres had still not been taken, it had now been brought within range of German artillery on three sides, effectively eliminating it as a base for an offensive. Captain Schwink in the OHL history pays tribute to the defenders at this point in the battle. 'The fact that neither the enemy's commanders nor their troops gave way under the strong

Men relaxing underneath the church clock at the newly set-up canteen in Poelkapelle near Ypres.

pressure we put on them, but continued to fight the battle around Ypres, though their situation was most perilous, gives us an opportunity to acknowledge that there were men of real worth opposed to us who did their duty thoroughly.'

War volunteer Paul Hub was one of those who had been involved in the decisive action General von Fabeck had called for. It was his unit's first action. 'I have lived through such horror recently, no words can describe it, the tragedy all around me. Every day the fighting gets fiercer and there is still no end in sight. Our blood is flowing in torrents. The first and second battalions only have 250 to 300 men left, so more than half are gone. Today only a few of my comrades will be still standing. My company commander, Lieutenant Massbauer, had been at the front for one hour when he was shot through the head. Pale and close to death, he was carried past me. Today, Sunday, I stood at his modest grave and joined in a prayer.'

Like many others, he had volunteered on the first day of the war, thinking it would be over quickly and that there would be few casualties. After his first experience of action, he wrote to his fiancée to explain what it was like at the front. 'All around me, the most gruesome devastation. Dead and wounded soldiers, dead and dying animals, horse cadavers, burnt-out houses, dug-up fields, cars, clothes, weaponry – all this scattered around me, a real mess. I didn't think war would be like this.'

As well as continual danger, there was the problem of sleep, keeping clean and replacements. 'We can't sleep for all the noise. At least thirty shells explode at once, the whole

Original caption 'German field watch in front of Antwerp.'

time. We called for back-up yesterday and today – I hope they make it. There are only a few of us left to tackle the English. I managed to wash myself properly yesterday, for a change. My beard is getting ever longer.'

Like Hub's regiment, *16 Bavarian Reserve*, in which Hitler was serving, had been decimated, but it was still sent briefly into action at Messines. Its third battalion was disbanded and the surplus shared between the other two battalions. It would be Christmas before the battalion could be reconstituted. After four days, Hitler's regiment 'had lost more than two-thirds of its combat troops, killed, wounded and taken prisoner.' To replace the fallen NCOs, men with a few hours' battle experience were promoted. In that same period, Hitler 'had been transferred from an infantry company to become a regimental dispatch runner, promoted to corporal and nominated for an Iron Cross.' He was not awarded the medal but, in a later battle against the French at Wytschaete during November, he was nominated for and awarded the Iron Cross Second Class.

On 1 November, Messines was abandoned, the French counter-attacks were mainly held, and the Kaiser went to Courtrai on a visit to resting cavalry divisions. At midnight, the bombardment of all trenches and buildings in Messines and Wytschaete began. An hour later, nine battalions of *6 Bavarian Reserve Division* advanced against Wytschaete. 'At the same time a general attack, in several lines, developed against Messines Ridge between the windmill…and Wytschaete.'

By fighting in the dark, the attacking troops could infiltrate through gaps in the British lines and by 0735 hours they were in possession of the middle part of Messines Ridge. At 0900 hours the British evacuated Messines. Wytschaete fell even earlier to the assault. By 0245 hours the leading troops had pushed their way into the village, forcing the British back to the southern and western edges. Initial counter-attacks by British and French troops were unsuccessful but, at around 0800 hours, they forced the Bavarians to pull back and abandon the village. Towards noon the Bavarian troops renewed their attack and by 1600 hours had entered the village only to be repulsed shortly after.

The fighting on 1 November was not restricted to the Messines-Wytschaete area. There were attacks along the front from the River Lys in the south to near Dixmude in

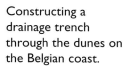

Constructing a drainage trench through the dunes on the Belgian coast.

the north. Success was somewhat limited across the front: Poezelhoek Château was taken, near Zillebeke British troops pulled out of a salient, and Messines was occupied.

2 November was to be another day of hard fighting. A new division and a fresh brigade were brought up to renew the attack and all along the front the bombardment of Allied positions was heavier than before. The battle was to be continued along the whole of *Fabeck's Army Group's* front.

By the end of the day some progress had been made at Veldhoek, Douve Farm had been taken and Wytschaete, where many of the inhabitants refused to leave even during the shelling, was finally captured, but overall by the end of the day there was little overall change. The official bulletin was more up-beat about the day: 'the attacks on Ypres are progressing. Over 2,300 men, mostly British, were taken prisoner and several machine guns captured'. The battle would continue the next day with a push against the Kemmel high ground by a newly created corps under the Duke of Urach, consisting of *3* and *26 Infantry Divisions*, newly arrived from France.

There was little change in the situation at the front over the next three days. However, the increase in the number of heavy guns and ammunition allotted to *Army Group Fabeck* permitted a heavier and increasing bombardment of Allied positions. Although Ypres was heavily shelled and the attacks continued, they were nowhere as heavy as in the preceding days. While the rumours spread among British and French troops that troops were being sent to Russia to alleviate the situation there, '*Supreme Command* was bringing up more troops for the decisive blow.' Writing after the war, General von Falkenhayn stated that 'it seemed as though it only needed perseverance in the offensive to obtain a complete success.' More troops were required.

By 3 November, troops released from duty by the inundation in the north had moved south and the forces of the *Fourth Army* had been reorganised. Crown Prince Rupprecht had concluded that Fabeck would not succeed without even more men, so he combed out men from across his command. He also ordered the following units to join *Fabeck's Army Group*: *Bavarian* and *2 Cavalry Division*, *25 Reserve Division* from the Flanders area, *4 Division* from La Fère which went to Lille, *9 Reserve Division* from Verdun and two *Guards*

A British POW column including walking wounded, marching to the rear.

Brigades from Picardy. The troops in the Guards Brigades were of superior physique and bearing and a minimum of five feet six inches tall. More heavy artillery was also given to the group as well as 'all the artillery ammunition allotted to the *Sixth Army*.'

French attacks during 3 November achieved no success. Indeed, near Bixschoote their line was pushed back. Throughout the day the British line was shelled and sniped but not attacked. The next day was very misty and from 1700 to 2300 hours it rained. Apart from the usual artillery activity it was quieter than the previous day and, for a second time, French attacks achieved no success. During the day Rupprecht received an order from the *Supreme Command* 'to push the attack immediately north of the Comines-Ypres Canal, and to put in all available forces to break through there'. However, the offensive could not wait for all the distant forces

A forward unit of French marines fighting near Ghent shipyards.

to arrive, for 'no time was to be given to the enemy to recover or to strengthen his positions.' The night was fairly quiet but on 5 November the shelling increased.

As more reinforcements were arriving, the French continued their attacks the next day. The attack on Messines, scheduled for 0700 hours, was delayed by the non-arrival of troops until 1500 hours. During this time *121 Infantry Regiment* and *122 Fusilier Regiment,* although shelled by the British and French guns, attacked and drove the French from Spanbroekmolen (Höhe 75) and advanced a further kilometre, claiming to have taken 300 prisoners. The French counter-attack did not recover the ground.

Neither was the French attack at Messines successful; it met a similar fate and did not recover the position. Near the coast, another attack by the French 42 Division failed; near Bixschoote, an attack was barely contained by the French who gave up some ground – but the potential casualty numbers were too great to risk pursuing this. The 1917 *OHL* Official History of the battle of Ypres admitted that the attack had been a failure and that a continuation of the offensive 'would have only meant a useless sacrifice of life.' The decision was made 'with deep regret, to resort to the long and wearisome task of sapping'.

6 November, like the previous day, found the French attacks failing to make progress. Fortune favoured German arms again. Across the front, Allied positions were bombarded and attacked but the more serious efforts were made near the Menin Road and either side of the Comines Canal. While the attack on the Menin Road, although initially successful, was eventually pushed back, the assault on French positions near the Comines Canal was more productive and brought the Germans within two miles of the walls of Ypres, threatening the Allied lines of communication and any retreat from the north.

The day had proved to be critical for the Allied Armies. As night arrived, the attackers

The last houses in Kruiksiek in use as billets and stables.

were 'in possession of Zwarteleen and close to St. Eloi, both less than two miles from Ypres. A deep wedge had been driven in at the junction of the French and British lines'.

As the new day dawned, once again visibility was limited by mist but this did not stop the artillery from shelling both Armentières in the south and Ypres in the centre of the front, the latter being set on fire in many places. With considerable fighting along the front, throughout the day, neither side made any real gains. The purpose of the series of small attacks the Allies were experiencing was to prevent them from resting and improving their defences; all the time the attacking force was increasing in size as reinforcements arrived.

Artillery fire the next day, 8 November, was heavy but less accurate because the weather made artillery observation difficult. As before, the bombardment of Allied positions continued throughout the day and vigorous infantry attacks were made along the front; the order was 'to attack somewhere every day.'

The constant artillery fire was seen by some as worse than going over the top. It was random and erratic, killing, maiming and destroying. Writing home from a trench on Hill 59 near Ypres, Lothar Dietz explained the problems: 'For the last three hours a corporal has been lying in a dug-out, with one arm and both legs shattered by a shell. The boyau (a trench or ditch covered with a parapet that provides communication between two trenches, particularly the rear and front lines. Boyaus were typically constructed in a zigzag pattern to prevent exposure to direct enemy fire from the front) runs down so steeply that it is impossible to carry him that way in a ground-sheet, and the other communication trench is under water...anyone who is badly wounded generally dies while he is being got out of here.' Each day saw a fresh crop of casualties from the artillery: 'today has cost us four killed, two dangerously and three slightly wounded'.

Private Aldag, writing home at Christmas, noted the state of the British trenches. A month earlier Dietz had told his parents why the English wanted their trench: 'Only 60 yards away from us are the English, and they are very much on the alert as they would be only too glad to get back our hill. We have a fairly decent trench up here, because we

Refugees returning to Malines from the south after the fighting had stopped.

drain all the water into the English trenches lower down, but our neighbours on the left, the *143rd*, have to keep two electric pumps going night and day, otherwise they couldn't escape the wet'.

Throughout the day heavy but localised fighting took place. The only serious attack was made by *143 Infantry Regiment* and part of *54 Reserve Division* north of the Menin Road, against the woods in front of Veldhoek Château, which provided good cover from view. Here the front was defended by both French and British troops. Attack was met with counter-attack and by the end of the day both sides remained roughly where they had started.

Although small in scale, all improvements in position were bought dearly. Oberleutnant Lentz of *Infantry Regiment 143* was involved in these small scale battles. 'Towards 5.00pm there was an intense battle, telephone lines were shot through and it was difficult to make ourselves heard. *Infantry Regiment 143* made some progress to the left of the main road, but there was no success to the right of it.' After a heavy howitzer bombardment, a

French colonial troops captured in the early days of the war in Flanders. They are being escorted to the rear by a solitary Landsturmmann.

reserve division tried to get forward but without success. 'Attempts to persuade the reserve division to get forward or to go into reserve behind our right flank also foundered.'

Losses were heavy, as Oberleutnant Lentz recalled: 'Oberst[Leutnant] Linker, *Infantry Regiment 143,* was killed during an assault designed to encourage the reserve division to press forward. Our slight success was bought dearly. Prisoners, both British and 4th Zouaves, were taken. They [were members of] Royal Fusilier, Lionhardt [sic], Lancastire [sic], Duke of Wellington, Grenadier Guards, Scotts Guards [sic], Badford [sic], Norfolk and 4th Reserve Battalion 4th Zouaves. However, despite all efforts and all the casualties, the wooded edge west of Veldhoek could not be reached.' A later attempt to storm the wood met with the same result and even higher casualties. 'The *Leib* Company of *Footguard Regiment 1* was reduced to nine men and *3rd Battalion Regiment 'Franz'* [Grenadier Guard Regiment 2] was completely wiped out in the woods.'

The next day was an uneventful day of minor Allied attacks that gained little. Moving to the front, Major Schering, Commanding Officer of *3 Battalion Grenadier Guards Regiment 2* saw an unusual sight: 'We reached Menen on 9 November. Further along the main road we could see a high ranking officer wearing the uniform of *1st Dragoon Guards*, his staff around him. As we got closer we saw that it was the Reichschancellor von Bethmann Hollweg.'

The *Guards* were classed as 'crack' troops who had been in action since the start, almost always on critical parts of the front. One more blow, using these élite troops, might bring about a decision in favour of the German Army. The *Guards* were rushed to the Ypres front.

As soon as he arrived from the Arras front, Major Schering quickly realised that it was not going to be easy to break the Allied line and that fighting conditions there were not the same as around Arras. 'Everywhere there were rubble heaps and ruined buildings, abandoned trenches full of bodies and the intensity of the bitter fighting was underlined by the presence of huge shell holes everywhere… We also made the unpleasant discovery that, in contrast with the situation around Arras, the high water table here meant that the mud was almost unbelievable.'

The trenches at Dorfeld.

Belgian troops with a requisitioned cart in a farmyard during the early days of the campaign. A Belgian propaganda card that was sent by a German gunner serving with *Field Artillery Regiment 68* in *40 Infantry Division*, to his wife in Leipzig in April 1915.

They found that long range shelling made movement difficult; to get to the front meant moving gradually from one less shelled area to another to eventually arriving at the destination. Nor was it easy to relieve troops in the front line. In many cases, the British trenches were only a short distance away and the roads were swept with machine gun fire. Moving along ditches was not an option either as 'they were full of corpses.'

In the dark, Major Schwerin's battalion found it very hard to relieve *Infantry Regiment 143*. 'The trench was very deep and festooned with heaps of corpses, over which we often had to climb. In some places the whole trench was covered with boards or doors, so it was like moving through a tunnel… Countless wounded men had dragged themselves into them and, in fear that we may tread on them, called out to us piteously.' The guides got lost; as men moved over ground, they just vanished, eventually arriving noisily at their destination hours late.

They were ready for the attack, and were relieved to hear, when the order arrived, that it would take place the next day. Even so, they were surprised by unexpected moments. In the dark, they found themselves opposite men with huge heads; these turned out to be Indians wearing turbans. As it became light, they realised that a British machine gun could fire almost straight into their trench. Around midday they captured a British corporal. While the major was interrogating him, a Zouave wearing a woollen hat pushed through the hedge and peered into the trench. "Don't shoot! I am the father of a large family with many children!" he shouted. At almost the same instant, he grabbed a water bottle from one of the men and drained it, much to the amusement of the grenadiers.

As early as 8 November, having previously informed the Kaiser that the army was exhausted, Falkenhayn had had an 'inner change'. Ten days later he suggested to the Chancellor that it was 'now time to develop a political strategy to detach Russia from its western allies.' Although Falkenhayn responded to Hindenburg's request for more troops to be sent to the east, the fighting around Ypres would continue. While Falkenhayn may have changed his mind about Flanders he was determined that his armies would hold steady: 'Hold on to what you have and never surrender a square foot of that which you have won.'

10 November was a comparatively quiet day along the front; this did not however mean that there was no fighting. Both sides attacked and defended with varying results. French attacks were anticipated and driven back. However, in the Dixmude area, after hand-to-hand fighting, the French and Belgian battalions were driven across the Yser; the destruction of the bridges over the Yser effectively stopped the attack. A French attack at Lombartzyde resulted in the gain of only a small piece of ground, but a Belgian effort against St. Georges, Schoorbakke and Tervaete achieved nothing.

In this sector, as the weather deteriorated, conditions became increasingly difficult as trenches filled with water. There was insufficient shelter for those in reserve forcing them to bivouac on sodden fields and, as so many troops had been sent south to the Ypres front, there were insufficient men available to effect regular relief of the front line. Conditions were just as bad on the other side of the wire.

Behind the front line the conditions were far from ideal and many places still bore the signs of battles fought weeks before. Six hundred yards behind Dietz's trench on Hill 59 was their reserve position, a small wooded valley that had been the scene of 'the most frightful hand-to-hand fighting'. The trees and bushes had been torn to pieces by shells and all about in the shell holes were bodies. Dud shells had made holes in the ground and there was French equipment lying about.

The capture of the Yser bridgehead was not the only success of the day. All the attacks and the intelligence gained by the Allies indicated a decisive attack to the north against the French, especially as the gains during the day were from the French: the cross-roads north-west of Bixschoote, occupation of 'the Kortekeer Cabaret and some trenches west of Langemarck', while the French 38 and 42 Divisions and a cavalry corps sustained considerable losses as they were pushed back.

One of those who fell that day was Alfred Buchalski from Bromberg, a philosophy student at Geissen, who was killed near Kortekeer. Not long before the battle he wrote home to describe what it was like at the front: 'With what joy, with what enthusiasm I went into the war, which seemed to me a splendid opportunity for working off all the natural craving of youth for excitement and experience! In what bitter disappointment I now sit here, with horror in my heart!

Belgian cavalry dismounted to act as an advance guard and ambush advancing German scouts.

How shall I ever properly describe to you the experiences of the last few days? I should like to give you a complete picture of the whole battle, but only little isolated incidents thrust themselves into the foreground. It was ghastly! Not the actual shedding of blood, nor that it was shed in vain, nor the fact that in the darkness our own comrades were firing at us – no, but the whole way in which a battle is fought is so revolting. To want to fight and not even be able to defend oneself! The attack, which I thought was going to be so magnificent, meant nothing but being forced to get forward from one bit of cover to another in the face of a hail of bullets, and not to see the enemy who was firing them!'

Original wartime caption: 'English infantry near Antwerp waiting for the enemy. In the foreground is a machinegun.'

The preceding attacks led the Allies to believe that the assault was being delivered to the north-east of Ypres. Reserves sent north to counter this left a weak French sector near the Comines Canal and the Zillebeke road. Generally, although the rest of the front remained quiet, minor attacks continued on British and French positions, gaining nothing.

The Allies knew that there would be an offensive and had predicted where they thought it would fall, but they did not know when; nor could they know that it had been postponed a day. The decisive attack should have started on 10 November 'when the new divisions had got into position and another strong reinforcement of engineers would have arrived'. To assist the attack, the newly arrived *4* and *Guards Division* became a new Corps and with *XV. Corps* formed the new *Army Group Linsingen*.

With the *Fourth Army* attack being postponed for a day, Major Schering's men spent the time organising themselves within their trenches and ranging in on the trenches of the enemy. During the day their orders for 11 November arrived.

The order commenced with a report on recent successes; details of the attack then followed. '*Fourth Army* has captured Diksmuide (sic) and crossed the canal south of Diksmuide (sic) in several places, taking 2,000 prisoners and six machine guns. In the area of Hollebeke numerous French soldiers have deserted to us. *XIX Corps* has beaten off the bitterly contested attacks of the British. A captured order is encouraging French soldiers to endure a few days longer in their trenches, by which time the attacking power of the Germans will have been reduced considerably. This order is an indication of how exhausted the enemy is already.'

The troops were informed that: 'Tomorrow at 10.10 am there is to be a general assault' preceded by an artillery barrage. However, 'should there be any sign before that time that the enemy is withdrawing then attacks are to be launched without waiting for artillery preparation and are to be driven forward with the utmost energy.' Schering's guards

A view of the damage done to the houses in Louvain after the mass burning of 25 August.

would not attack alone: 'All neighbouring formations will be participating in the attack.' A supplementary order gave further details: 'At exactly 10.00 am, by synchronised watches, artillery fire is to cease. This sudden silence by our artillery is the signal for our entire forward line of infantry to launch the assault.' Detailed orders were provided and map overlays showed each unit its approach to its final destination.

The decisive attack was to be made across the Gheluvelt front between the southern end of Herenthage Wood and the southern end of Polygon Wood. General von Linsingen was instructed 'to drive back and crush the enemy lying north of the Comines Canal', while *Army Group Fabeck* was to maintain its position west of the canal, continue to press forward and support the left wing of von Linsingen's forces. The remainder of the units of both *Fourth* and *Sixth Armies* 'were to attack with the utmost energy, so as to pin the Allies to the ground and allow them no rest'. However, the newly formed corps in *von Linsingen's Army Group* felt itself not fully prepared due to the weather conditions; the attack was postponed for *Sixth Army,* but the greater part of *Fourth Army* acted on their

Belgian ammunition carts being pulled by dogs. Many dogs were employed by the Belgian and French Armies at the start of the war. Although a neutral country, Holland also used dogs for the same purposes.

The night attack of the Prussian Guard on British trenches near Ypres. The sender, a soldier in *111 Infantry Division*, had served in Belgium where the division was formed in 1915, but at the time was fighting on the Artois front.

original orders and attacked the French between Langemarck and Dixmude.

Although the French had been attacked with considerable vigour during the day, the night was quiet, with no indication of what was about to happen. The decisive attack was to be made, Crown Prince Rupprecht's orders instructed, by *Fabeck* and *Linsingen's Army Groups* and *XXVII. Reserve Corps* on the left wing of *Fourth Army*.

The weather conditions the next day were not seen as the same by each side of the conflict. The *OHL* book, 'Ypres', records pouring rain in the morning and a rainstorm that beat in the faces of the attackers, while the British record the day as misty until noon, when it rained, but not heavily, until around 1800 hours. Regardless of the weather conditions, at first light, the artillery, reinforced the previous day, put down the most intense barrage the British had yet experienced; a barrage that increased in intensity as 0900 hours approached. Although the Allies had not known where the attack would be made, the volume of artillery fire indicated that it was to fall mainly on British positions.

Although it was to be a decisive attack, it did not go as planned. The assault near Messines did not even leave the trenches and throughout the day the line remained unaltered. Opposite French positions near the Comines Canal, the official account recorded 'slow but sure progress' and the capture of a 'battery of four machine guns' but the British account differs; it considers that there was 'considerable firing, but no change in the situation'.

North of the canal, the weakened French force held out until around midday when it was pushed back to Hill 60 and the outskirts of Verbrandenmolen by *30 Division*. It was a good start to the day, especially as the French had no immediately available reserves. However, the arrival of a French cavalry regiment and the resultant counter-attack pushed the attacking troops back. Although the French managed to establish a new line, it was less than two miles from Ypres.

The main attacks against the British resulted in severe casualties and in many cases gained little or nothing. One though was more successful, but still costly. In the Veldhoek area, the British had withdrawn from the front line in response to the heavy bombardment. As a result, when the shelling suddenly lifted, 'the *Fusilier Battalion* of the *2nd Guard grenadier Regiment* was able to reach and cross the trenches, which were protected only by a trip wire, before there was time to man them'. Pushing on quickly they advanced five hundred yards into the Veldhoek Woods, eventually reaching the château that was held by French troops. Although their advance was checked, it allowed *4 Guard Grenadier Regiment* to move forward. Like *2 Guard Grenadier Regiment,* their advance was also held. A charge by British troops pushed the attackers out of the wood, but not back to their start positions.

With the barrage not completely stopping at 1000 hours, any potential surprise was lost as Leutnant von Scheele of *4 Guard Grenadier Regiment* found when his company left their trench. 'I blew my whistle and launched myself forward. In order not to be recognised as an officer, I was carrying a knapsack and a rifle. Right and left of me the men were going down in rows'. He was one of the first to arrive at the British trench: 'The British were still firing at us, cutting us down, but some were surrendering. Only twenty five of my men succeeded in getting into the trenches. The remainder were all shot down, the two flanking platoons mowed down by machine gun fire.' They had captured the trench but were cut off and could not inform battalion headquarters.

A similar situation arose near Polygon Wood. Shortly after 0900 hours, when the barrage stopped, the first troops rose from their trenches; led by officers with drawn swords, silently, at the double, rifles at the port, they attacked the British positions. Crossing over the first trenches without firing, they attacked the defenders with bayonets, overwhelming the line but meeting such resistance that they began to lose their cohesion. Attempts to reinforce the attack failed because of British artillery fire.

In its regimental history, *1 Foot Guard* recorded the attack and the casualties: 'the companies in second line advanced over the captured trenches, received heavy fire from the right and turned against the strongly wired Verbeek Farm. Attempts to storm it failed, and the troops, like their neighbours, were forced to lie down and dig in'.

One of the two attacking regiments moved too far south, while the other turned off to deal with British troops in Polygon Wood, a target which should have been attacked by *XXVII. Reserve Corps* troops. This created a large gap between the two units, and, as

Trophies of war. English field guns captured near Ypres by Saxon troops on display in the market square in Leipzig.

A wayside grave at Boninne near Namur. 'True to the Fatherland until death, fourteen German Grenadiers rest here.'

a result of British shelling, the battalion detailed to cover this eventuality was unable to move forward. However, the assault had created a break in the British line through which the attackers moved so quickly that the British machine guns were overwhelmed before they could inflict many casualties. Nevertheless, overall casualties were heavy in *3 Foot Guard Regiment*.

Although the *Guard Corps* had not achieved its aim, its attack won praise from the British. 'The *Guard Corps*, in spite of having suffered severely in Belgium, of having been thrown headlong across the Oise at Guise, and of having lost large numbers on the plains of Champagne and on the banks of the Aisne, advanced against Ypres on November 11 as bravely as they did on August 20.'

In spite of the heavy fighting, the British managed to mount a counter-attack and by late afternoon had moved sufficiently far forward for the French to start shelling them, thinking they were German troops. By nightfall many of the attackers were close to where they had started the day, with some British units still trying to restore the line in the pitch dark. However the attacking troops still held the British front line from the Menin Road to Polygon Wood.

On the right wing, French attacks failed to recover any of the ground lost the previous day. Similarly, the heavy attacks made on French positions at Drei Grachten and Knocke also failed in their objectives.

Across the front, at the end of 11 November, the German Army was 'pressing in on Ypres on both flanks and in the centre.' The communiqué for the day's fighting read: 'In the neighbourhood east of Ypres our troops advanced further. A total of more than seven hundred French were taken, as well as four guns and machine guns.' Also mentioned was the attack of 22 October, referring to youthful regiments west of Langemarck singing 'Deutschland, Deutschland über Alles' as they attacked, and recording the capture of 2,000 French and six machine guns.

That night 'the weather was dreadful, with rain filling the shallow trenches and neighbouring shell holes more and more as time went by. The night air was filled with the moaning of those who had been severely wounded and, although stretcherbearers

Trenches in the late autumn of 1914 some distance behind the front line.

worked through the night to rescue them, many succumbed to exposure and a lonely death isolated between the positions.' Many would lay where they were, unburied until the snow covered them.

Rudolf Binding, who served in Flanders, was in command of an independent squadron of dragoons attached as reconnaissance unit to a newly formed 'Jungdeutschlanddivision'. He described what happened in his division: 'young fellows…only just trained, are too helpless, particularly when their officers are killed. Our light infantry battalion, almost all Marburg students…have suffered terribly from shellfire. In the next division, just such young soldiers, the intellectual flower of Germany, went singing into an attack on Langemarck, just as vain and just as costly.'

13 November was a Sunday and, even with a war going on around them, troops on both sides found time to attend church parade. Private Aldag described the experience in a letter home: 'at 10 o'clock, we had a Parade Service. A village church, which had already

A card for the Home Front to sweeten the reality – the lighter side of trench life.

served as a Field Hospital and was strewn with straw, was decorated with greenhouse plants and flowers. The Divisional Protestant Chaplain read a passage from the Bible and we sang a hymn "Follow me, Christians". Then came a sermon followed by the chorale "Now thank we all our God". It was a moving ceremony, full of thoughts of home.' A month later, Aldag was in French Flanders getting ready for the first Christmas of the war.

While Aldag was enjoying a church service, Dietz was desperate to get back to the front. 'Nine hundred men are just off from here to reinforce *105 (Regiment)* at the Front, with bands playing and church-bells ringing, and the tears are running down my face because I have to sit here doing nothing while my brave comrades out there are fighting so gallantly'. He had been wounded attacking 'that louse's nest Gheluveld, which had been fortified and was defended by 18,000 picked English troops, after we had captured two lines of trenches protected by the most awful barbed-wire entanglements and contact-mines. Out of the seventeen Deputy Officers who went to the front with me, five have been killed', he told his parents, 'and seven wounded'.

While the battle for Ypres did not end until late 1918, the first phase was over before this month was out; the exact date differed according to the army the soldier was in. For the French it ended on 13 November, for the British 22 November, and for the Germans 30 November, although to the latter it was all but over by 20 November. Indeed the idea of abandoning the offensive surfaced on 17 November. Ludendorff admitted that 'no break-through had been accomplished' and, although 11 November was hailed as a great success, von Moltke wrote to the Kaiser that the offensive had been an 'utter failure to be successful.'

Throughout the battles intelligence had been difficult to obtain, particularly in the coastal area held by the French and Belgians. On both sides estimates of the numbers of men opposing them amounted to no more than guesswork or incomplete calculations based on scraps of information. The day after Dixmude was captured by the Germans a Prussian officer was taken prisoner and interrogated. He asked his captors how many of them there had been. '"How many were you?...Forty thousand, at least?"' And, crying with rage when told that the marines were only six thousand strong, he exclaimed: '"Ah! If we had only known!"'

This photo clearly shows the problems faced by troops in the winter. As much of the land has a very high water level, bailing out trenches during rainy periods was a common event.

The following days saw serious fighting and POWs on 13 and 17 November stated that the attacks they were involved in were 'to be decisive and a decision was to be made at any price'. Their orders were to get to Ypres at all costs. However any attacks were held and little real progress was made. When the weather changed, the battle dragged to a halt. As a result of the heavy losses for little gain the Kaiser, on 15 November, was recorded as being despondent.

After days of cold and rain, the snow came on 15 November, followed by frost, then hard frost, then a snow storm. By 20 November, the ground was covered in snow. Trenches filled with water, frost-bite appeared and with the trenches so close to each other, rest was difficult: grenade-throwing and sniping were constant. The ground became a sea of mud in which men often sank up to their knees. In so much mud, weapons were hard to clean and tended to jam.

'Cold rain had muddied and even flooded many trenches, and decomposing bodies floated to the surface. Crude 'duckboard' platforms barely kept soldiers dry, but few were eager to shelter in mucky hideaways that might be worse. Unless soldiers moved about, they would sink into the liquefying mud, and many slept erect if they could, leaning against the dripping trench walls. It was a stomach-churning atmosphere for eating one's rations. Latrines were non-existent and accomplishing bodily functions a nightmare.' To Otto Dix the landscape was 'the work of the devil.'

Berlin Wireless Bulletins described the same conditions with comments on unfavourable weather, storms and driving snow resulting in trifling progress which might prevent success. Eventually the standard bulletin explained that in Flanders the situation was unchanged.

While the official explanation for the halt was the weather, the editor of the *Berliner Tageblatt*, a reserve infantry Leutnant serving in Flanders, wrote of the quality and hardiness of the opposition they faced in confronting the British: 'They soon gave us practical proof that they could shoot, for in the first few engagements our battalion was reduced to half.' The writer could find no fault with his opponents, stressing how able they were at all aspects of soldiering, their energy and their ability to defend and then counter-attack: 'we were at once struck with the great energy with which their infantry defended itself when driven back and by the determined efforts made by it at night to recover lost

A panoramic view of Ypres before the war.

ground…The main strength of the British undoubtedly lies in the defence and in the utilization of ground.' He also acknowledged the quality of both French and British artillery. In a similar vein but very briefly the British Official History shows respect for its opponents: 'The splendid discipline and high courage of the German troops may be freely admitted, for these qualities were exhibited in many a fight.'

Confirmation of the cessation of the Ypres battle is clearly given by the changes made to the Order of Battle by the end of the month: *III. Reserve Corps* under General Beseler, *XIII. Corps* under General von Fabeck and *II. Corps* under General von Linsingen along with all the cavalry were sent to Russia. Falkenhayn then wanted to attack a weaker area but there were no longer sufficient forces in the west to mount an offensive between Bapaume and Roye.

'This second bid for victory was costly and it also inaugurated static (trench) warfare.' However, losses on both sides had been high. The British Official History gives the total casualties from 14 October to 30 November as 58,155. German casualty returns were irregular, covered different periods and did not include wounds dealt with in the area so no exact comparison is available but between 18 and 30 October the battles for Ypres and the Yser resulted in 123,015 casualties.

By November 22, the Allied line in Flanders had been redistributed with the British holding a compact front from Givenchy, near the La Bassée Canal, to a point near Wytschaete, a distance of around twenty-one miles. On either flank were French troops who occupied the Ypres Salient. Included with the British troops was the Indian Corps.

After the battle for Ypres had finished, both sides were exhausted. General von Fasbender saw that he was now involved in siege warfare. 'We lie opposite one another for weeks, indeed months…we no longer know days, only months of continuous fighting. Open warfare has degenerated into a sort of siege warfare – without being siege warfare.' This was echoed in a letter home written by Stefan Schwimmer, a farmer from Württemburg: 'Those who are only at home cannot possibly imagine. There is no day, no night, no Sunday, no weekday.' The killing never stopped.

Exhaustion and poor weather led to a lull in operations but the sniping, shelling and bombing continued with varying degrees of intensity. Both sides were active at night: during the last week of November the British carried out several successful minor night

Death could arrive at any moment. A single heavy shell explodes in the distance.

A view of trench life. 'Trenches were not built in straight lines. This was so that if the enemy managed to get into the front line trench they would not have a straight firing line along the trench. Trenches were therefore built with alternating straight and angled lines. The traverse was the name given to the angled parts of the trench.' The traverse can be clearly by the heads appearing in the background.

operations but the Indian Corps could not contain an attack by *112 Regiment* that successfully captured 800 yards of trenches east of Festubert. However, this success was short-lived; the trench was lost to a counter-attack that lasted throughout the night.

Much time and effort went into digging a series of defence lines and erecting a considerable amount of wire, which required a lengthy period of quiescence in the fighting activities of most of the troops. Across no-man's land, the British were also digging, improving and connecting their trenches. 'The effect of artillery fire compelled them (both sides) to take cover in good trenches and behind thick breast-works. As the armament in use became more and more powerful, artificial shelter, where the surface water allowed it, had to be made deeper and deeper in the earth.'

The troops on both sides experienced the same discomforts, hardships and constant shelling. Those at home received the bland news that there was no change in the west and that, apart from artillery activity, all was quiet. In reality, though there was no major battle, it was anything but quiet. The real picture was not published, though the troops did express their fears, pain and hopes in their letters home.

Lothar Dietz, a philosophy student, wrote home in November from a dugout in the trenches on Hill 59, 2 miles south-east of Ypres: 'You at home can't have the faintest idea of what it means to us when in the newspaper it simply and blandly says: "In Flanders today again only artillery activity." Far better go over the top in the most foolhardy attack, cost what it may, than stick it out all day long under shell-fire, wondering all the time whether the next one will maim one or blow one to bits.

Six hundred yards behind here is our reserve position, a little wooded valley in which the most frightful hand-to-hand fighting has taken place. Trees and bushes are torn to pieces by shells and larded with rifle bullets. All about in the shell holes are still lying bodies, though we have already buried many.'

The burial of bodies was a problem everywhere at the front as another soldier noted: 'neither the dead nor the wounded can be removed. If you put up as much as a little finger above the edge of the trench, the bullets come whizzing round immediately. The dead

Another card designed to counter Allied accusations of German barbarity; inoculating the local population.

bodies must therefore be allowed to remain in the trench; that is to say, the dead man is got rid of by digging a grave for him in the floor of the trench.'

In reply to the regular bombardment of their trenches by pre-war design light, medium and heavy trench mortars which had been in use before the war, and the sudden arrival of stick grenades during raids or in attacks, the British improvised a number of home-made grenades and trench mortars of varying success.

In the front line it was not possible to worry about anything other than survival. Behind the lines troops used their skills to create a more peaceful reality. Lothar Dietz told his family: 'As one can't possibly feel happy in a place where all nature has been devastated, we have done our best to improve things. First we built quite a neat causeway of logs, with a railing to it, along the bottom of the valley. Then, from a pine wood close by which had also been destroyed by shells, we dragged all the best tree-tops and stuck them upright in the ground; certainly they have no roots, but we don't expect to be here more than a month and they are sure to stay green that long. Out of the gardens of the ruined châteaux of Hollebecke and Camp we fetched rhododendrons, box, snowdrops and primroses, and made quite nice little flower-beds.'

'We have cleaned out the little brook which flows through the valley, and some clever comrades have built little dams and constructed pretty little water-mills − so-called "parole-clocks", which, by their revolutions, are supposed to count how many minutes more the war is going to last. We have planted whole bushes of willow and hazel with pretty catkins on them and little firs with their roots, so that a melancholy desert is trans-formed into an idyllic grove.'

'Every dugout has its board carved with a name suited to the situation: "Villa-Woodland-Peace", "Heart of the Rhine", "Eagle's Nest", etc. Luckily there is no lack of birds, especially thrushes, which have now got used to the whistling of bullets and falling of shells. They wake us in the morning with their cheerful twittering.'

Another soldier who was thankful for any comfort was Johannes Iwer, Doctor of Philosophy, born in Berlin on 30.5.92 and who died near Het Sas on 28.4.15. 'You can form absolutely no idea of our incredible privations. But all the same my health is, thank God, quite satisfactory. When at night I have to crouch, in the bitter cold, with rain

A photo by Antony of Ypres showing the damage caused to the library.

streaming unceasingly down on us poor 'Field-Greys', keeping a sharp look-out on the enemy trenches, I just roll myself in a blanket and am thankful for my warm underclothing.'

While soldiers dug in, the Supreme Council concluded that the Flanders campaign was not achieving the required results. 'There was much criticism of Falkenhayn's conduct of the offensive, not least for employing badly trained reserve formations.' This was seen as a waste of a future resource especially as the casualties had been heavy. One influential officer described the casualties as 'useless deaths'. As a result of the failed offensive there were attempts to oust Falkenhayn but he was not replaced until August 1916.

Falkenhayn put forward two reasons for the lack of success: firstly, the Belgian inundation of a large part of the country as a defensive measure, and secondly, the constant stream of Allied replacements. The heavy losses around Ypres were difficult to replace: one reason for going on the defensive in the west was the aim to win the war in the east, where Austria-Hungary needed assistance to stay in the war. As a result, it was decided to send seven divisions and cavalry from Flanders to the east, to be followed in January by three newly-raised corps and an existing corps from France that would be replaced by a new one.

After 23 November, this decision to concentrate on the Eastern Front resulted in

A card to raise funds for the German Veterans league of the Army and Navy. The card shows the routing of the British forces at Antwerp by German Marine soldiers.

transports moving some troops to the rear while others, the majority, marched to the railhead. Some columns were caught by British artillery fire. *26 Infantry* and *48 Reserve Divisions* left the Flanders front, with *26 Infantry* going to Poland. Other units followed, leaving two corps, *VII* and *XIX (Saxon), 6 Bavarian Reserve*, a quarter of *II Bavarian Corps* and *29 Infantry Division* facing three British Corps and the Indian Corps. 'The continuous bad weather in the autumn and winter in this water-logged country caused great suffering', so much so that troops leaving for the Eastern Front were much envied.

Further north, four corps and a *Landwehr Brigade* faced four French Corps and two unattached divisions, and in the coastal region one army corps and the *Marine Corps* faced the Belgian Army and a French territorial brigade. The *Marine Corps*, a naval unit, fought in the trenches as soldiers, guarded the coast against landings and used torpedo boats, submarines and aircraft. Apart from those on the coast, there were considerably more French and British troops than German ones.

'By the end of November, the German Army was incapable of any further offensive

Comparison photographs to show the damage caused by the first bombardment of the Cloth Hall in Ypres.

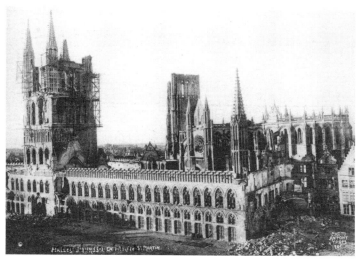

action. The war to date had exhausted the German Army.' Nearly half its field strength were casualties. On the Western Front the troops 'were so weary of battle that on some occasions during the Ypres offensive officers had to drive their men at pistol point out of the trenches into the attack.' Ammunition reserves needed to be built up and the army rested before any further operations could be mounted. December was to be a quiet month in which to rebuild the army. On the other side of the wire the Entente had other plans. The next offensive would be a British and French attack, Warneton to Messines and Wytschaete to Hollebeke respectively.

The operations between 14 to 24 December are known as the 'December battles in Flanders' but, to the British, constituted the 'Attack on Wytschaete'. They were a response to what the British saw as a weakening of German defensive capacity and the gaps that had arisen from the troop movements. As they left their trenches on 14 December, the French and British troops met with considerable resistance; the French made no progress, while the British got as far as the deep wire; only one unit got through to the first trench where they took forty-two men of *5 Bavarian Reserve Regiment* prisoner. As Wytschaete and the wood to its west did not fall, no further attacks were made, and shelling only brought down heavier retaliation on the British and French lines.

The positions that the French and British were attacking were strongly protected by practically intact wire and by nature herself, in the form of hopelessly deep mud. Although operations were continued over the next two days, the attempts were half-hearted and no positions fell. By the end of 17 December, the French, using a sap, had advanced only 100 yards on the Menin Road; equally slight progress was made near Klein Zillebeke and Bixschoote.

With such little success, the French moved their main efforts to Arras and later the Champagne region, while the British assisted by making diversionary attacks in Flanders. This attack floundered because of fog, and any support that the French and British might have provided was curtailed by a counter-attack on French positions in front of Ypres.

The British continued with minor attacks along the front, in some cases making small territorial gains which were generally lost within a few hours to counter-attacks and/or the impossibility of consolidating the positions because of the water-logged ground. In

By the onset of winter both sides had entrenched. As the Germans held the higher ground, their trenches were often drier. Newly constructed trenches near Ypres in 1914.

the close fighting, the superiority of the offensive stick-grenade became apparent.

In mid-December the British mounted a series of small but costly attacks intended to provoke aggressive responses. 'The most expensive failure, at Ploegsteert Wood – "Plugstreet" to soldiers in the field – on 18 December, resulted in massive casualties, including many from poorly directed friendly artillery fire. Many of the dead remained unburied, some literally impaled on enemy barbed wire.'

As Christmas drew closer the men's thoughts turned to more peaceful activities. Private Aldag wrote home on 18 December to describe his unit's activities. 'I have been singing our Christmas hymns with great delight and moved by the most devout feelings. We sing them in two parts in our rest billet, a big warm cow-house, with, on the one table, a little lit-up Christmas tree which somebody has had sent from home...On Christmas Day I shall be at home in thought with you all the time.'

Shallow trenches at Bixschoote, autumn 1914, showing a sandbag parapet to protect troops on the fire step.

While Aldag's comrades made their Christmas preparations the war went on. That night he had to sleep in "Alarm Order" – in their packs with all equipment strapped and buckled on – a very uncomfortable experience in itself and in addition, to disturb their attempts at sleep even more, throughout the night 'there was a tremendous noise of gun and rifle-fire.'

Although both sides agreed on the centrality of Christmas, neither of them expected what was to come – a let-up in the war. Commanders were becoming aware of a 'live-and-let-live' attitude that seemed more prevalent now the weather had worsened. Neither side was firing at mealtimes, and while neither side openly fraternised, friendly banter crossed the lines and, where lines were especially close, newspapers weighted with stones were thrown across to each other. And even before Christmas there had been truces to bury the dead. The level of fraternisation had reached such a point that it was strictly forbidden by the British II Corps.

With the transfer of many units to the Eastern Front 'a disproportionate number of German units were now undertrained and unenthusiastic Bavarian, Saxon, Hessian and Westphalian reservists', most of whom 'would have rather been home for the holidays' and who 'evidenced little hate.'

A precursor of what was about to happen over Christmas occurred a week earlier in French Flanders. A splendid chocolate cake was slipped into the British lines with a message: 'We propose having a concert tonight as it is our Captain's birthday, and we cordially invite you to attend – provided you will give us your word of honour as guests that you agree to cease all hostilities between 7:30 and 8:30…When you see us light the candles and footlights at the edge of our trench at 7:30 sharp you can safely put your heads above your trenches, and we shall do the same, and begin the concert.' The invitation was accepted with an offer of tobacco, and at the appointed hour a "double quartet" of whiskered heads popped up and sang "like Christy Minstrels".'

On 19 December Ludwig Finke, a law student from Leipzig in Saxony, arrived in Flanders. He recorded his experiences in a letter home that day. 'A warm wind from the sea rustles softly through the leafless treetops and almost drives the breath back into one's lungs. How long have we already been marching in the still moonlight? There are riders on the country road. A troop of refugees passes almost without a sound; the children whimper softly, their elders creep by hollow-eyed, with faces of dumb misery. We are getting near the Front. Smashed-up carts, ammunition-wagons. Here and there a dead horse which lies with its legs stretched out and its neck sunk into the boggy ditch which separates meadow from road. Then the dead warriors'.

These dead warriors were lucky enough to have been buried near where they fell. Many were just left in no-man's land, in shell holes or where they died in trenches. In the trenches many were used to improve the trench walls or buried underfoot when time could be made to deal with them. Men who had 'seen too many horrible things all at once' tended to be hardened beyond their years. 'A few days ago…a soldier was so badly hit by a shell that he was cut in two…[his shattered body] could not be removed without risk to the survivors and was therefore allowed to remain'. Even in cold weather, bodies tend to putrefy and he 'gave rise to a horrible stench and whatever they did the men could not get away from the mutilated, blackened features. Sometimes arms and legs torn away from the body are allowed to lie about the bottom of the trench' until someone could be bothered to bury them.

Finke's first night in the trenches is lit by a distant burning farm but all is quiet until morning. As he stretches, a bullet aimed at the spike on his helmet throws sand into his face as a warning to remain still. Then the artillery starts up on both sides. 'Louder and louder come the crashes and between them the humming and whistling in the air.'

Like Private Dietz, Finke did not like the uncertainty of the shelling. The first shell landed ten yards away, damaging the roof of a house. He wrote to his parents explaining

Captured Belgian field artillery being removed for transport and use in Germany.

how it felt to be caught in a barrage; 'then follows the slow seeking of the enemy guns for us; that calm, sure eating of their way nearer and nearer which affects one's nerves till one trembles like thoroughbred horse which hears the crack of a whip close by'. The only answer was to stay cool and light a pipe.

Being near the sea may have seemed pleasant upon his arrival but Finke soon learned that this was not always so. The next night he was in a nearby pine forest in the rain. As they moved between the trees his column was held up and he could hear the word 'water' from in front. 'It came suddenly. It gushed out of the ground. The sea had broken through again. We wade through water, first knee-deep, then up to our waists, then again up to our knees. One's coat gets very heavy. One man has lost his boots. On again... One man suddenly stumbles and plunges into the water. Curses and low laughter, for at a first glance the effect is comic. Comrades help

Lightly wounded British POWs captured near Ypres in a café in Lille on their way to Germany.

him out'. Not knowing where they were going, they kept marching, and slowly but surely the sound of the guns grew faint.

By 20 December the British and French had ceased major operations, leaving Corps staff to execute low level local operations. While they were winding down, retaliation came in the form of an attack against a weak spot in the Allied line. At daylight on 20 December, the whole front of the Indian Corps was severely bombarded by heavy artillery and trench mortars, followed by ten small mines, driven out in sap-heads, exploding near the British lines at Givenchy; there was also an infantry assault by two battalions of 57 Regiment and four engineer companies on a 900 yard front. Although much of the newly captured territory was eventually taken by British counter-attacks, an area around Festubert held out.

As a result of the attacks, the Indian Corps was removed from the line and sent into reserve. Against losses of around 250 killed, the attackers claimed to have taken nearly 1,000 POWs. The fighting that occurred during this period was accepted by OHL as the heaviest fighting on the Western Front during the winter of 1914/15.

To the German General staff, the first battle of Ypres was a victory because they had stopped the Allies falling on the rear of their western forces, preventing them capturing the rich industrial north of France. The Belgian coast also offered a base for naval operations against Britain. For the Entente, the battle was also a victory. It had held and stopped a German advance against the Channel Ports, which provided rapid access to the continent.

Military police inspecting the damage outside the Hotel Majestic in Ostend, the result of naval shelling.

There may have been a war on but the troops were preparing for the Christmas holiday, 'bringing up small trees and holiday provisions.' At home, 'promoted by newspapers, commercial enterprises packaged *Liebesgaben*, or loving gifts…At the front as real *Weihnachtsbäume* were emplaced, the troops, especially the Saxons, attempted to decorate them, no easy matter in trench conditions, although the weather was becoming more Christmas-like.'

British officers worried about the suspension of military deliveries for twenty-four hours in order to bring 355,000 Princess Mary Christmas tins to the front because they believed that all the Germans thought of was war. In this, they were way off the mark. On the other side of the wire the same was happening. Instead of a box, other ranks received 'a large meerschaum pipe with the profile of Crown Prince Friedrich Wilhelm on the bowl, or a box of cigars inscribed *Weihnacht im Feld, 1914*. Noncommissioned officers got a wooden cigar case inscribed *Flammenschwert* – a flaming sword.'

The amount of gifts sent by public subscription was very generous. Dominik Richert in French Flanders recorded the contents of his *Weihnachtspakete* as including among the many gifts 'chocolate, sugarbread, sweets, cigars, cigarettes, Dauerwurst, sardines, whistle, suspenders, gloves, muffler'.

So much was given that it generated a 'semi-official' dispatch – 'A Christmas Onslaught onto the Field-Grey: Yesterday about four-o'clock in the afternoon there was a fierce and terrible onslaught of Christmas packages onto our trenches. No man was spared. However, not a single package fell into the hands of the French. In the confusion, one soldier suffered the impaling of a salami two inches in diameter straight into his stomach…Another had two large raisins from an exploding pastry fly directly into his eyes…A third man had the great misfortune of having a full bottle of cognac fly into his mouth.'

Indeed, so much had been sent that transport and supply depots were seriously disrupted. At the front, officers complained that crowded billets and narrow trenches were becoming dangerously congested with goods and parcels. However, within days of its receipt, the food would be gone.

On 23 December, 2 Cameronians were surprised to see their enemy bailing out their

The grounds of Schloss Hooge after the fighting had finished.

trenches, fully exposed and waving their arms to show they had no weapons. No shots were fired. Nearby another British unit allowed two of the enemy to come over to exchange cigars and greetings in English. It turned out that one of the two Germans was a Birmingham cab-driver who wanted the war to end so he could go back to his job.

There was no let-up in the death and destruction, even though the battle for Ypres had ended and Christmas was not far away. Writing to his parents on 26 December, Ludwig Finke told them about his awful experiences up to Christmas Eve when he was able to put forty-eight hours of horror behind him – a time when nobody believed that they would ever get home again. On 23 December he was sent off to fetch rations. When he got back his dug-out had received a direct hit.

While he had been lucky, his comrades had not. Henn, the man with whom he shared the dug-out, 'was dead, lying up to the waist in rain-water, his skull smashed and a splinter in his back. He was sitting just as he was when I left him a quarter of an hour before, his rifle on his arm. My dear neighbour…had two bad wounds. Altogether we lost eight killed and 37 wounded out of 85!' With no cover, his sergeant, corporal and four other men helped him dig a new home.

The same day as Finke's misfortune, men of *16 Bavarian Reserve Regiment* (the regiment Adolf Hitler served in) were feeling fortunate. They had been relieved and were heading

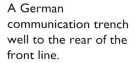

A German communication trench well to the rear of the front line.

for a rest in a ruined monastery at Messines. Having settled into the comfort of the cellar, they set up a Christmas tree (thousands had been delivered to the front) and brought all the beer sent to them by breweries across the country. As night fell, nearby Saxon troops began placing Christmas trees on the parapets of their trenches with candles clamped on. Intrigued British troops, followed by their officers, soon crawled out to find out what was going on. This impromptu cease-fire led to an informal truce over Christmas Eve and Christmas Day.

For the whole of Christmas Eve, Finke stayed in the dug-out with his Sergeant-Platoon-Commander, both chain smoking and counting the shots to pass the time. The sergeant had been out since 8 August, fought at Dixmude and on the Yser, but had not been in an almost incessant forty-eight hour barrage. 'Then came the star-lit "Holy Night", and our Christmas music was a horrible blending of the screams of the wounded, the whistling of rifle-bullets and the bursting of shells.' Then they were relieved by a unit that had not been in the line before. Fortunately the British did not attack.

Hitler was probably the only man in the regiment who was not happy with the truce. For the remainder, 'it was a holy time from the 22nd to 29th December [and] the regiment had no losses in dead and wounded to mourn. As Tommy himself kept totally quiet.'

Along the front arrangements were made to make it a 'You no shoot, We no shoot' day. 'Signboards arose up and down the trenches in a variety of shapes. They were usually in English, or – from the Germans – in fractured English…YOU NO FIGHT, WE NO FIGHT.' It was not just English troops who fraternised, in some areas both the French and Belgians joined in.

The truce was also a time to attend to urgent business in many parts of the front – burying the dead. 'In daylight, the Christmas cheer was inhibited by the decaying shapes of the dead, some mercifully covered by new snow.' Parties soon got to work burying the dead and quickly men from both sides got to know one another. In many cases this retrieval of corpses and their burial were preconditions for fraternisation.

On Christmas Eve the French attacked Bixschoote with no success. The next day was Christmas and the unexpected happened. For many in Belgium the war stopped. Writing home, Aldag told his parents what had happened in his area. 'The English had been singing hymns, including a fine quartet. On our side too the beautiful old songs resounded, with only now and then a shot in between. The sentry-posts in the trenches were decorated with fir-branches and tinsel from home, also the dug-outs.'

The temperature dropped and the freezing cold put an end to the mud and filth. In

Marine soldiers digging in near Fort Waelhem in Antwerp.

The coastal towns with their docks and marine facilities provided the German Navy and air force with bases from which to prosecute their attacks on England.

front lines and rest areas throughout Flanders troops received their Christmas mail. 'It was delightful to see the men all standing together while the names were read out and the parcels handed out over their heads. They were all real "Christmas children" as they knelt before the packages and burrowed into them.' For Private Aldag this happened by a manger in a cow shed – as on the first Holy Night.

One commonly reported occurrence was football, usually without a real ball although Kurt Zehmisch of *134 (Saxon) Regiment* recorded in his diary that the English somehow had one in their trench. It did not matter who won. It was playing the game that was important; a game that was wonderful and strange at the same time. As a result of a match with a kilted battalion, their opponents soon learned the truth about what Scotsmen wore under their kilts: 'the Scots wore no underpants under their kilts so that their behinds became clearly visible any time their skirts moved in the wind.'

Well behind the line, Finke's unit had a peaceful Christmas Day. They were able to sleep for seven hours and eat their fill. Then the snow came. Forgetting they were going back into the line the next day they drank to each other's health and to those at home.

For many units the real Christmas celebrations took place in the evening. For Aldag's company 'there were two big trees, standing all lit up on big tables. We got everything we could possibly wish for: knitted comforts, tobacco, cake, chocolate, sausages – all "Love-Gifts". What Germany has done for us! Then the Colonel and the Divisional Chaplain came in, the Bible story of Christmas was read and the dear old hymns were sung.'

Private Aldag was still out of the line over New Year enjoying the comparative comfort of a cow-shed when he wrote home about the truce. 'An English officer came across with a white flag and asked for a truce from 11 till 3 o'clock to bury the dead (just before Christmas there were some fearful enemy attacks here in which the English lost many in killed and prisoners). The truce was granted. It is good not to see the corpses lying out in front of us anymore.'

With the business of removing the dead completed, the truce should have come to an end; but incredibly it was extended. Then to everyone's surprise 'the English came out

A captured English trench near Ypres.

of their trenches into no-man's land and exchanged cigarettes, tinned-meat and photographs with our men, and said they didn't want to shoot any more. So there is an extraordinary hush, which seems quite uncanny. Our men and theirs are standing up on the parapet above the trenches.'

The situation could not be allowed to continue for too long so Aldag and some men were sent across to tell them to get back into their trenches as they were about to restart firing. 'The officers answered that they were sorry, but their men wouldn't obey orders. They didn't want to go on. The soldiers said they had had enough of lying in wet trenches and that France was done for.'

During this encounter Aldag realised he was better off than his enemy: 'they really are much dirtier than we are, have more water in their trenches and more sick.' He did not realise who he was fighting against, supposing them to be mercenaries on strike because of their poor conditions. Regardless of who he thought they were, neither he or his comrades were keen to shoot, preferring to walk about in the open. Again reflecting a lack of hard

A camouflaged dug-out entrance in a damaged house near Ypres.

feelings in the war, Aldag's officers went over and signed an English officer's album.

The truce ended the next day when an English officer went across to convey the information that the High Command had ordered an artillery barrage on this section. Telling them to take cover, he returned to his lines to be followed by French artillery firing on the German lines. Although violent, the shelling caused no casualties. Along the front the war returned, and the killing started again.

With Christmas now a memory, thoughts turned to the coming new year and once again to family. Private Rohweder wrote home on 29 December: 'I dream so often of you. Then I see our house in the moonlight. In the sitting-room a light is burning. Round the table I see your dear heads: Uncle Lau is reading; Mum is knitting stockings: Dad is smoking his long pipe and holding forth about the war. I know that you are all thinking of me'.

The truce was not mentioned in the despatches from France. Its partially truthful version of the day read: 'On Christmas Eve a hard frost set in, and the 25th was very cold, though it was not bright, for a mist hung over the countryside. On our right… we captured a short length of trench. It was also discovered that a group of buildings behind the German front line was being used as headquarters of some sort…fire…was therefore concentrated on the spot. In our centre the only incident was the capture of two of the enemy, who came across to our trenches uninvited, ostensibly to wish us the compliments of the season. Boxing Day was quiet except for some shelling by the enemy of a few points near our left…On Sunday…nothing occurred.'

Manpower was becoming a problem for both sides. The British regular army had been decimated, with losses of over 100,000 men, and the French had suffered nearly one million casualties. With under 700,000 casualties on the Western Front, the German Army had suffered less but Germany's population was smaller than those of her two main enemies. Belgian losses were under 50,000.

The manpower shortage was further compounded by von Falkenhayn's 'change of plans and the operations in Russia had led to eight infantry and six cavalry divisions being withdrawn from the Western Front during the last two months of the war to reinforce' the Eastern Front, which had also claimed twelve of the newly-formed divisions created at the depots after the start of the war from reservists, ersatz reservists and volunteers. By

A mounted Hussar patrol on the outskirts of Kruiseik during autumn 1914.

the end of the first month of 1915, the number of divisions facing the Allies was ninety-eight as against 106 at the beginning of November 1914. There were no immediate reinforcements available apart from the Class of 1914, which had provided enough men to bring companies up to around 180 men, sixty below their war establishment; it was estimated that a corps was only at eighty per cent of its establishment.

Not only did the operations on the Eastern Front take away much-needed manpower from the west, but also a large quantity of artillery, ammunition and materiel. After limited local attacks against French positions in France, the army was 'compelled to adopt a purely defensive attitude in' both Belgium and France. The offensive now appeared to have passed to the Allies. However, 'as soon as the corps had been brought up to strength after their losses in the battles of Ypres…the reduction of the…Ypres Bridgehead…was taken into consideration by the *Fourth Army*.'

'The failure at Ypres had far-reaching consequences. First, the inability to break through the primitive Entente trenches meant that mobility could not be restored to the front.' However, if they were not broken in the near future they would only become increasingly sophisticated and more difficult to breach. 'Second, the failure of the offensive and the high casualties caused Falkenhayn to rethink fundamentally German strategy.' Although many pressed for a decisive attack in the east, already plans were being made for a further offensive on the Ypres front.

Any new attack would be very different; the army now had the advantage of a new weapon, poisonous gas. This weapon had been experimented with during October for use in shells, but as the output of these shells was insufficient, delivery from canisters was authorised.

The possession of Ypres by the Allies appeared to offer them possibilities for an offensive towards Brussels and Lille. Its capture would shorten the line, allow the last section of Belgium to be conquered and threaten the Allied flank. The idea of a two-army assault fell through, leaving *Fourth Army* to set its own targets and come up with its own resources.

Reinforcements brought companies close to strength and, after looking at the options, the proposed *XXVI. Reserve Corps* plan was decided upon – the capture of Langemarck

Mass produced postcard for the Homeland showing soldiers and field gun in position in front of the Justice Palace in Brussels.

and Pilckem ridge with the eastern bank of the canal as far up as the Boesinghe railway bridge. Once decided upon, 'preparations for the attack were immediately taken in hand. Besides the collection of material, a normal gauge railway to bring up super-heavy guns was constructed through Houthulst Forest, and narrow gauge lines were laid up to the front; sidings and huts were built and roads improved by Belgian labour. None of these significant measures came to the knowledge of the Allies.'

There was a major problem with gas: it relied upon the wind being in the right direction, which might take some time to occur. The vagaries of the weather meant that the gas might well have to be in position in the trenches, together with the troops taking part in the attack, for an indefinite time; every day would increase the chance of its discovery by the British.

Aldag's unit had returned to the front line for the New Year but, as at Christmas, neither side felt the need to ruin the moment. 'On New Year's Eve we called across to tell each other the time and agreed to fire a salvo at 12. It was a cold night. We sang songs, and they clapped (we were only 60-70 yards apart); we played the mouth-organ and they sang and we clapped.'

Auf Befehl S. M. des Kaisers „den Verwundeten und Kranken der deutschen Armee im Operations- und Etappengebiete gewidmet vom als Weihnachtsgabe" Central-Comitee der deutschen Vereine vom Roten Kreuz.

A card sold to raise money for the Red Cross Christmas appeal showing the Kaiser in the field on active service. It was sent by a soldier in *7 Field Hospital* in *Fourth Army* somewhere in Flanders.

When Aldag asked if they had any instruments, they replied by playing their bagpipes. As arranged, at 2400hrs both sides fired a volley into the air. Although a few artillery shells were fired and Very lights were sent up, Aldag and his comrades waved torches and cheered. For the occasion they had brewed some grog and were able to drink a toast to the Kaiser and the New Year. He wrote home to tell them that 'it was a real good "Silvester" (New Year's Eve), just like peace-time!' Aldag was killed two weeks later near Fromelles in French Flanders.

In his diary, artilleryman Sulzbach recorded his thoughts, which typified those of many others, on the end of the year. 'So 1914 is winding up today. A year to raise your spirits, but also a year of pain and sorrow, not only for us but for the whole of what is called the civilized world. This terrible war goes on and on, and, whereas you thought at the start that it would be over in a few weeks, there is now no end in sight'.

'An hour before midnight on 31 December the fusillade of fire that blazed from the German trenches was all that the most ardent advocate of the offensive spirit could desire' – but not the British troops, who were enjoying a quiet life in the trenches oppo-

With the first Christmas of the war close many units produced their own individual cards to celebrate the event. This *XXVI. Reserve Armee Korps* Christmas postcard of Rumbeke Château was sent to Flensburg.

site. When the shells passed over their heads they realised that this sudden resumption of the war was a celebration of the New Year on Berlin time.

The results of the fighting in 1914 vindicated the expectations of no one. 'Schlieffen's plan was in ruins' and the enemy's armies were still in the field, 'in positions that could henceforth only be attacked frontally'. As both sides said goodbye to 1914, the stage was set for the first gas attack on the Western Front in 1915 and the date of that would be decided primarily not by Generals or soldiers but by the wind.

Chronology of the Flanders Front – 1914

3 August Cavalry cross into Belgium at Gemmenich.

4 August War declared on Belgium. Invasion begins on 15-mile front and includes attack on the fortress city of Liège. Cavalry take Visé, eight miles north of the city and ford the River Meuse north and south of the city. Belgian Army concentrates behind the River Gete to the west of Liège.

5 August Demand for free passage through Liège rejected by Belgian Government. Surprise night attack on Liège by six composite brigades fails to capture any of the twelve forts. Namur reached by cavalry patrols.

6 August *14 Brigade* failed to take Liege forts after night assault. Situation saved by arrival of Ludendorff who tries a different approach, personally leading the men through gaps between the forts but forts continue to resist. French Sordet Cavalry Corps cross into Belgium with King's permission and get to within 9 miles of Liège. Zeppelin raid on Liège forts.

A Red Cross collection card to support the work of the wartime volunteers who were assisting the wounded.

7 August	City of Liège falls giving troops river crossings but forts continue to hold out.
8 August	Belgian Army retreats towards the River Dyle. Fort Barchon in Liège falls after intense shelling and Headquarters mistakenly announce that all the Liège forts have fallen but fighting continues.
9 August	French cavalry enters Belgium. BEF lands in France.
10 August	Two super-heavy siege mortars are transported from the Krupp Works at Essen to Liège to bombard the forts.
11 August	Fort Evegnee surrenders. Advancing troops clash with Belgian infantry at Tirlemont, St Trond, and Diest.
12 August	Two 420mm howitzers shell Liège forts. Attack on Haelen repelled by dismounted Belgian cavalry. Huy falls. First German pilot killed on active service. OberLeutnant Jahnow, a veteran of the 1912 Balkan war who flew for the Turkish air force killed in a crash near Malmédy.
13 August	Austrian 305mm howitzers shell Liège and three forts surrender (one blows up).
14 August	Two more Liège forts surrender.
15 August	Liège forts fall and garrison commander General Leman is taken prisoner in ruins of Fort Loncin while unconscious. *Richthofen's 1 Cavalry Corps* repulsed during attempts to cross River Meuse south of Dinant.
18 August	Tirlemont captured as Belgian Army retreats towards Antwerp Battle of Gettes, with further fighting at Grimde and Hautem St. Marguerite.
19 August	Defeat at Aerschot by Kluck forces Belgian Army to retreat from River Gette towards Antwerp. Louvain taken and Aerschot destroyed with 150 civilians shot. Siege of the nine Namur forts begins with 2,700 Belgian troops facing five divisions.
20 August	Victory parade through Antwerp by *IV. Corps*. Belgian Army withdraws into Antwerp Fortress. *II. Corps* sent by Kluck to invest it.

The peaceful town of Aerschot before the war.

21 August	Heavy bombardment of Namur begins at 1000 hours. Battle of Charleroi along River Sambre forces river crossing and forces attacking French divisions back eight miles.
22 August	*4 Cuirassiers* in the first action against British cavalry near Mons. British main force west of Monsot Tournai as intelligence reported. First RFC aircraft shot down by German rifle fire in Belgium.
23 August	Six divisions, one after another, moving in text-book fashion, blunder into British positions and are decimated by accurate rapid small arms fire resulting in 4,000 casualties. Attacks by Hausen's troops against the French successful and troops cross the Meuse at Dinant.

Besides the 42cm mortars used to shell the forts ringing Amsterdam, the city was also attacked at night by Zeppelins.

24 August	As a result of the previous day's fighting the French pull back, followed by the British retreat from Mons. Namur is entered. Three Namur forts fall.
25 August	Last three Namur forts fall to heavy artillery barrage. Belgian night attack recaptures three villages south of Malines but later troops move out.
26 August	Last two Namur forts fall. French First Army falls back and British fight a day-long delaying action at Le Cateau.
31 August	Naval Corps formed to garrison Liège and later the Belgian coast.
9 September	Capture of Antwerp ordered by the Kaiser. *IX. Reserve Corps* halted by Belgian attack.
15 September	RFC start their photographic reconnaissance of the Western Front over Belgium.
17 September	Battle of Malines-Aerschot ends and Belgian Army retires on Antwerp.
22 September	Rail communications cut in three provinces by 700 volunteer Belgian cyclists from Antwerp.
26 September	Siege of Antwerp begins and Malines shelled. Push southwest of Dendermonde and Scheldt held by Belgian troops.

27 September	Troops enter Malines. Siege train of 173 guns and 175,000 troops deployed against Antwerp fortifications.
28 September	Malines falls. Super-heavy howitzers bombard Waelhem and Wavre-Ste. Catherine forts in the outer ring of the Antwerp defences, causing magazines to explode.
29 September	Antwerp bombardment intensifies: Forts Koningshoycht, Lierre and Kessel heavily shelled.
1 October	Fort Waelhem taken and Belgian counter-attack driven off. Royal Naval Division lands at Antwerp.
2 October	Forts Koningshoycht and Lierre abandoned by Belgian garrison. Termonde taken.
3 October	British promise to assist Antwerp defences as outer defences have now fallen.
4 October	Belgian 4 Division holds attack by *37 Landwehr Brigade* on Scheldt. Over 200 British Marines arrive to assist Antwerp garrison.
5 October	Four battalions cross the River Nethe at Duffel. French troops sent to assist the Antwerp garrison are halted at Ghent by General Pau.
6 October	Lierre taken and Belgian Army begins to evacuate Antwerp.
7 October	Four brigades cross the River Scheldt and threaten the evacuation of Allied forces but Belgian forces hold the vital Lokeren railhead. *IV. Cavalry Corps* reaches the outskirts of Ypres.
8 October	*IV. Cavalry Corps* passes through Ypres but is stopped by French Cavalry Corps under Mitry ten miles from Hazebrouck. Further fighting and heavy bombardment in Antwerp result in damage to over 200 houses, the capture of two inner line forts and the retreat of the Belgian 2 Division and British troops behind the Terneuzen Canal north of Ostend.
9 October	Inner defences of Antwerp taken and nearly a thousand British troops taken prisoner. Burgomaster signs ceasefire treaty at *Beseler's HQ*.

Trenches near Langemarck with soldiers in occupation.

The shelling of Ypres often continued into the night. An artist's impression of the bombardment of Ypres, using mortars.

10 October	Antwerp formally capitulates with Belgian commanding officer offering his sword at Fort Ste. Marie; the garrison had previously decamped. Attack on Ghent held by defending Belgian troops.
11 October	Start of a six week struggle for control of the Channel ports with the Belgian Army reforming around Bruges. Cavalry forced back to the River Lys by British cavalry.
12 October	Allied troops evacuate Ostend and Zeebrugge. British attack on an eight mile front at Messines and force their way through to Givenchy.
13 October	British troops occupy Ypres with two French Territorial Divisions moving in to reserve positions west of the town. Belgian troops driven out of Ghent.
14 October	Bruges captured. British cavalry reach Kemmel and Messines linking with British infantry.
15 October	*III. Reserve Corps* occupies Ostend and Zeebrugge. Belgian Army digs in along the Yser River. Allied line now extends to the North Sea and occupies Poperinghe. Although British cavalry find garrisoned River Lys crossings, they lose two villages on the Ypres Canal. British II Corps troops held by newly arrived *VII. Corps* that was to relieve *Cavalry Corps*.
16 October	Battle of the Yser begins with an attack on Dixmude; Belgians retire from Houthulst Forest to the northeast of Ypres. Allied forces occupy Aubers, Neuve Chapelle, Givenchy and Warneton. The BEF crosses the River Lys and advances up to three miles, with its 7 Division digging in five miles east of Ypres.
17 October	Allied offensive ends with the capture of Herlies and entry into Armentières. The new *Fourth Army,* with eight newly formed divisions along with *III. Corps* from Antwerp and the *I Marine Division* begins its advance towards Yser and Ypres.
18 October	Successful day: Roulers captured, British Cavalry Corps attack thwarted and two Belgian outpost villages captured by *III. Reserve Corps*. A Royal

	Navy flotilla of two cruisers, four destroyers and three monitors shell German positions east of the River Yser.
19 October	First battle of Ypres begins against British and French troops across the front from the channel to Armentières. HQ flying corps (*Fleigerkorps der Oberstein Heeresleitung*) formed at Ghistelles near Bruges.
20 October	*Fourth* and *Sixth Armies* attack between La Bassée Canal and the North Sea, aiming to break through between Ypres and Nieuport and envelop the northern flank of the Allied armies and roll them up. *III. Reserve Corps* storms Lombaertzyde village east of Nieuport. Kaiser arrives at Courtrai ready for the taking of Ypres. *Sixth Army's* attacks on the La Bassée to Messines front repulsed as the British I Corps goes into the line near Ypres but Passchendaele ridge is successfully occupied.
21 October	Seven divisions face the Belgian Army. Dixmude falls and the Battle of Langemarck starts with British troops holding a line from Zonnebeke – St. Julien – Langemarck – Bixschoote. French lay mines off Ostend to deter U-boat movement.
22 October	Belgian 2 Division re-enters Lombaertzyde but night attack by *III. Reserve Corps* pushes Belgian troops back. The Yser is bridged near Tervaete, the village taken and the bridgehead expanded. British trenches stormed north of Pilckem. British dismounted cavalry before Messines stiffened by arrival of two Indian Army battalions.
23 October	Pilckem trenches lost to British attack. Heavy fighting around Langemarck. *45 Reserve Division* receives heavy casualties attacking British positions near Ypres. French troops arrive in Ypres to replace British. French 42 Division containing many veterans of the Marne enters the line near Nieuport. Ostend bombarded by the Royal Navy; fire directed by balloon.
24 October	Polygon Wood positions fall to British attack. French positions in Dixmude attacked repeatedly throughout the day but no progress is made even after fifteen attacks. A French counter-attack northeast of

Die Kämpfe in Westflandern.
Nachtgefecht im Überschwemmungsgebiet bei Nieuport.

The fighting in West Flanders as seen by a war artist for the Leipzig Illustrirten Zeitung. British searchlights provide illumination during a night attack in which the defenders fight hand-to-hand with the attackers across the destroyed bridge at Nieuport.

Ypres fails to make progress but Zonnebeke is lost and French soldiers hold the village despite a six-division attack. Allied naval squadron on Flanders coast increased to two cruisers, thirteen destroyers, one gunboat, two monitors and thirteen sloops.

25 October   Belgians open Nieuport sluices at 1600 hours to flood the area east of the Nieuport-Dixmude railway. British and French positions attacked all over the Ypres Salient but British intelligence had picked up orders being radioed by the Corps commander in plain language.

Josef Hummel was killed in action on 29 October 1914 while serving in Flanders with *1 Company 5 Infantry Regiment*. Had he lived to his next birthday, 8 December, he would have been twenty-eight.

26 October   Fierce fighting on the Yser.

27 October   *III. Reserve Corps* with *Naval Division* attack Belgian Army. Falkenhayn visits Sixth Army HQ. Six divisions form the newly created *Army Group Fabeck* to the south of Ypres.

28 October   Eight battalions of *14 Division* enter Neuve Chapelle and capture Krusik south of the Ypres – Menin Road. French attack north of the Ypres – Roulers railway gains little and defenders inflict over 2,000 casualties.

29 October   *Bavarian 6 Reserve Division* repulsed east of Gheluvelt.

30 October   Zandvoorde and Hollebeke captured. Initial assault on Belgian lines successful in gaining two villages and breaking the Belgian 2 Division, but four Allied battalions penetrate back into Ramscapelle, forcing troops back due to waist-high water behind them stretching over a width of 2,000 to 3,000 yards.

31 October   Second phase of the battle starts at 0900 hours with smaller scale assault made between Messines and north of Gheluvelt. *Army group Fabeck* consisting of seven fresh divisions are tasked with breaking through at Ypres and rolling up the enemy's line on both sides after a 700 gun three hour earthquake bombardment. Just as the breakthrough is imminent, ten enemy battalions hold the attack, charge and rout over 1,200 soldiers in Gheluvelt château. Nine battalions successfully infiltrate on to Messines Ridge and French troops are driven off some of the ground to the north of the ridge. French reinforcements arrive to strengthen positions north of Ypres and 7 Indian Division arrives to bolster British lines. British start to use London buses to transport troops around the salient.

Ehre dem Andenken
des tugendsamen Jünglings
Joseph Auer,
Schuhmachermeisterschn v. Ering,
Soldat im Ersatzres.-Inf.-Reg. Nr. 17,
welcher im Alter von 23 Jahren bei
einem Sturmangriff auf Wytschaete am
1. November 1914 sein junges Leben fürs
Vaterland geopfert hat.

Fürs Vaterland u. seine heiligen Gesetze
Gabst du dein junges Leben hin:
Ein größrer Lohn als alle Erdenschätze
Wird dir dafür im Himmelreich erblühn.

Druck von J. Lehner, Simbach a. Inn.

Joseph Auer, a master shoemaker's son from Ering in Bavaria. He was killed in a charge at Wytschaete on 1 November 1914 at the age of twenty-three while serving with *Ersatz* (replacement) *Reserve Infantry Regiment 17*.

1 November British positions in Messines and Wytschaete taken but assault is stopped by French troops to the west of the attack area. Adolf Hitler, an unknown Austrian soldier, serving in the *List Regiment,* is promoted to Lance-Corporal (Gefreiter).

2 November The battles of Armentières and Messines end, as the focus moves to taking Ypres, and troops west of the Yser are withdrawn except from two villages which repel the French attacks.

3 November Allied troops move forward to occupy abandoned positions on the Yser.

4 November Lombartzyde falls to Allied troops.

6 November Attack against British positions at Klein Zillebeke fails and further ground lost to their attacks. The Kaiser visits positions at Menin.

7 November British positions at Givenchy attacked and Lombartzyde retaken.

8 November Fighting along the whole front from Dixmude to Arras.

9 November Fierce attack on British positions at Ypres. Falkenhayn forms a new army group under General Linsingen to take Ypres. *U12* is the first U-boat to enter Zeebrugge base.

10 November The Battle of the Yser ends with heavy fighting along the northern end of the Flanders Front. Over twenty divisions attack Ypres and *43 Reserve Division* storms Dixmude, but French manage to blow the bridges before the capture.

The banks of the Yser canal between Boesinghe and Lizerne. On the left German soldiers' graves, to the right captured French dug-outs.

11 November Battle of Ypres enters its third phase: the Battle of Nonne Boschen . Third attack, in thick mist, using a fresh corps of over 17,000 soldiers of the *Prussian Guards* and *4 Division* from Arras, pushes down the Menin Road (Gheluvelt to Ypres). Troops break through British positions north of the road but hesitate to push further, unaware that British guns face being overrun. British scratch force of cooks, engineers and batmen, stiffened with just over 300 regular infantry, repeatedly counter-attack and push the *Prussian Guards* back.

12 November Official communiqué on the previous day's fighting reports that: 'In the neighbourhood east of Ypres our troops advanced further.' A total of 700 French were captured as well as Hill 60.

13 November Pressure on the Allied positions lessens.

14 November Troops' fighting ability reduced by severe shortage of artillery shells – only four days' supply.

15 November British troops gradually replaced by French with British not taking responsibility for the salient again until early 1915.

16 November Heavy rain and flooding swamp the Yser battlefield.

17 November Low fighting strength, transfers to the Eastern Front and bad autumn weather bring *Fourth Army* attacks to an end.

19 November Fighting limited to artillery duels and infantry skirmishes.

22 November First Battle of Ypres ends with desultory local attacks on British positions.

23 November Cathedral and Cloth Hall damaged by heavy artillery battery. Zeebrugge shelled by two British battleships.

25 November Sniping posts at Garfeld farm near Ypres blown up by the British.

26 November Unsuccessful attack on Yser canal falls.

30 November Artillery duels but no infantry action.

2 December Troop-carrying rafts on the Yser near Dixmude destroyed by enemy artillery fire.

4 December Langemarck positions taken by French.

6 December Fifteen inch naval guns fire on Dunkirk from positions twenty miles to the east.

Wervik is a border town on the River Lys. The picture was taken from the French side of the border just before the war.

10 December	Attacks against British positions in the salient unsuccessful.
13 December	Troops pull back from Yser Canal.
14 December	Two French divisions attack near Klein Zillebeke and British troops make headway in Petit Bois to the south of Wytschaete.
15 December	Enemy Nieuport Group forces cross the Yser towards Lombaertzyde. Terrain in much of the salient is now a quagmire.
16 December	Westeinde bombarded by Royal Navy.
17 December	Enemy positions in Armentières bombarded.
18 December	U5 hits a mine and sinks close to the Flanders coast.
21 December	First confirmed attack on the United Kingdom by air takes place. A Friedrichshafen FF29 floatplane of the German Navy's *See Flieger Abteilung 1 (Seaplane Unit No.1)* dropped two bombs on Dover Harbour, both of which fell into the sea.
23 December	Belgians cross the Yser south of Dixmude.
24 December	Many units fraternize with the enemy during the Christmas truce. The first successful bombing attack on a target in the United Kingdom takes place. A second Friedrichshafen FF29 floatplane of *See Flieger Abteilung 1* dropped a single 22 pound bomb, which blew a crater 10 feet wide and 4 feet deep in the garden of a Dover resident. There were no casualties. Two British aircraft were scrambled in response to the attack but the aircraft was not intercepted.
25 December	Unofficial Christmas truce continues on land. During an attempted attack on the London dock area, a Friedrichshafen FF29 floatplane of *See Flieger Abteilung 1* was intercepted over Erith by a Royal Flying Corps Vickers Gunbus based at Joyce Green. During the pursuit the FF29 released 2 bombs, which landed in a field near Cliffe railway station. The Gunbus crew broke off their attack when the aircraft's solitary Vickers-Maxim machine gun jammed and, although damaged, the FF29 succeeded in returning to base near Zeebrugge.

27 December	Trenches near Lombaertzyde lost to Belgian attacks.
28 December	St Georges near the Yser lost and all recovery attempts fail.
30 December	British spend the day consolidating their positions.
31 December	Artillery active on both sides from the Yser in the north to Verdun in the south.

Histories of the Divisions that fought in Flanders

Military history is mostly written about the movement of units, some large, some small, with personal experience added where relevant, but rarely dealing with the history and origin of the troops involved.

Unlike the British Army, apart from the initially war-raised service battalions and the Territorial units, the German Army was rigidly territorially based so that divisions had a regional flavour. Again, unlike Allied divisions, they were quality and age related, providing attack, defensive, holding, Russian Front and line of communication divisions, with the best troops being siphoned off into the storm troop divisions. Furthermore, unlike the British, many German divisions stayed on the same front for many months, or even in some cases for years, a factor which afforded them an intimate knowledge of their combat zone. Each division had a history and often an ethnicity that could make it a better choice for a particular situation than another of the same age group and social background. Allied intelligence naturally kept a close eye on the make-up, history and combat-worthiness of each division, maintaining a full record on each on the Western Front.

The German Army was not a single entity. The Prussian Army, at eighty per cent of the personnel in the army, was the major component, but even in itself was not a single entity. Serving in its ranks were troops drawn from the Grand Duchies of Baden, Hesse, Oldenburg, Mecklenberg-Schwerin, Mecklenburg-Strelitz and Saschen-Weimar, the Duchies of Anhalt, Saschen-Altenburg, Saschen-Coburg-Gotha and Saschen-Meiningen as well as the principalities of Lippe, Schaumburg-Lippe, Schwarzburg-Rudolstadt, Schwarzburg-Sonderhausen, Waldeck-Pyrmont and the two Reuss states. Also administered by the Prussian state were soldiers from the Imperial Lands of Elsass-Lothringen, the state of Brunswick and the Hanseatic Free Cities of Bremen, Hamburg and Lubeck.

The Kingdom of Bavaria was second in importance and fiercely independent.

Completing the German Army were the troops of two semi-independent states: Saxony and Württemberg. While Bavaria and Saxony had their own officer corps, in times of war all independent armies were subordinated to the Prussian Army that then controlled training, equipment and organisation. But this did not stop the rivalry between these states and Prussia. There are many recorded instances of departing troops, who had kept the sector quiet, sending messages to the enemy telling them the Prussians were coming and to give them Hell.

An infantry division consisted of two infantry brigades, an artillery brigade and a cavalry regiment. As the troops came from specific areas, many of them had names as well as a number; *25 Infantry Division was* known as the *Hessian Grand Ducal Division,* while *40 Infantry Division* was alternately *4 Saxon Division.* In the same way many of the infantry regiments had two designations: regimental number in the army and then a territorial number; some had a further title that showed something about their history. Hence, *Infantry Regiment 169 was* also *8. Badisches Infanterie-Regiment* from Baden, *Infantry Regiment 126* was known in Württemberg as *8. Württembergisches Infanterie-Regiment Nr.126 (Grossherzog Friedrich von Baden* and *Infantry Regiment 36* was also *Füsilier-Regiment General-Feldmarschall Graf Blumenthal (Magdeburgisches) Nr. 36.*

The constitution stipulated that while the standing army should not exceed more than one per cent of the population, every male was liable for service over a twenty-seven year period from the close of his seventeenth to forty-fifth year of his age. At the age of seventeen he was enrolled in the 1st Ban of the Landsturm, but was not called to active service until he was twenty. After two years with the colours, three years in the cavalry and artillery, and five and four years respectively with the reserve, at the age of twenty-seven he transferred to the 1st ban of the Landwehr for five years, to the 2nd Ban for seven years and finally at the age of thirty-nine he passed into the 2nd Ban of the Landsturm where he remained until his forty-fifth year. There was always an excess of recruits over the peacetime establishment, so nearly half of the potential intake was turned down for service and were simply added to the muster rolls of the 1st or 2nd Bans of the Landsturm or, if aged between twenty and thirty-two, were posted to the Ersatz Reserve.

This structure gave the German Army a large reserve of trained soldiers in the time of war to add to its regular establishment of around 35,000 officers and over 650,000 NCOs and men: a reserve, an Ersatz Reserve, a Landwehr formed from trained soldiers and a Landsturm of untrained youths and middle-aged ex-soldiers. The latter were for duties inside the German frontiers but, as casualties mounted, many found themselves transferred to other types of formation. As a result of this, within a week of hostilities breaking out, nearly four million were serving with the colours, of whom over two million were deployed on the Eastern or Western Front.

With a population of over sixty-five million, the army was able to expand rapidly initially from ninety-two divisions at the start of the war to over 200 by the armistice. A brief history of those divisions that fought in Flanders is detailed below.

This record of divisions gives a clear indication of the speed of movement in the first few months of the war, and shows how quickly divisions moved from one front to another according to the needs of the advance or retreat. It also demonstrates that as things settled down into trench warfare, divisions stayed in an area for long periods of time,

A card sent by a member of *Pioneer Miner Company 292* in *54 Reserve Division* to Frau Olga Voigt. It clearly illustrates the unpleasantness of life in the trenches during the winter months with deep water and mud slides.

some for most, if not the whole war, whereas, in the British Army, divisions moved along the front from army to army on a regular basis.

The Flanders front is often cited as being very active, but during certain periods it was much quieter than other parts of the front. While the battle of the Somme was taking place, the Flanders Front was a place to send divisions to rest and re-fit before going back. This record details both the transient and permanent divisions on the Flanders Front.

I Bavarian Landwehr Brigade

After fighting in the Vosges, *I Bavarian Landwehr Brigade* was detached at the beginning of October and sent to garrison Antwerp, where it stayed until December. It then returned to the Champagne region and did not return to Belgium.

I Guard

Composed of regular troops, the division left Prussian Wallonia on 11 & 12 August and entered Belgium, crossing the Meuse at Huy on 18 August. On 23 August, it fought at Fosse and St. Gerard, after having crossed the Sambre at Jemmapes. Fought at Fournaux on 24 August and was engaged on 29 August between Guise and Vervins. After fighting on the Marne and near Hebuterne, *I Brigade* was sent to Gheluvelt in Flanders to rest before being sent to the Champagne region.

I Guard Reserve

At the beginning of the war, *I Guard Reserve*, together with *3 Guard*, formed the *Guard Reserve Corps* that swept into Belgium as part of *Second Army* under von Bulow, on 16 August, crossed the Meuse at Ardenne on 20 August where over 200 inhabitants were massacred on the same day and pushed on as far as Namur. On 29 August the corps was pulled from the line and sent to East Prussia on 1 September.

2 Guard Reserve

Recruits for the division came from Westphalia and Hanover. At the beginning of the war the division was grouped with *19 Reserve Division* in *X. Reserve Corps*, forming part of von

Bülow's Second Army. The division left Zulpich on 10 August and arrived in Belgium four days later, passed the Meuse near Liege on 17 August, surrounded Namur on the north, crossed the Sambre to the west of Charleroi on 22 August, and fought at Marbaix the next day before moving to France.

1 and 2 Naval

The division entered Belgium on 4 September, detrained at Brussels and two days later joined the corps besieging Antwerp. After Antwerp fell, the division marched along the coast and by 23 October had arrived in the area between Bruges and Ostend. On 2 November it relieved *4 Ersatz Division* in front of Nieuport St. Georges.

On 24 November the *1* and the newly formed *2 Naval Division* formed the *Naval Corps* with the specific function of guarding the sea front and coastal sectors of occupied Belgium. *1 Division* was responsible for the seafront from Raversyde to the frontier of Zeeland as far as Maldegem, while *2 Division* controlled the front on land from the North Sea to Schoorbakke, four kilometres southeast of Nieuport.

Rifles propped against the trench wall; a soldier sleeps while another sits. A picture of mundane everyday life in a trench.

The personnel of the divisions were Marine or Sailor Fusiliers recruited from the seamen or general population of the port towns of Germany and were classed as being of mediocre fighting value.

3 Guard

In August the division was sent to the Western Front where it fought below Namur. On 27 August it was sent east for the invasion of southern Poland. It did not return to Belgium until late in 1917.

3 Infantry

Recruited in Pomerania, the division, along with *4 Division*, formed *II. Army Corps* from Stettin. In August the division formed part of *First Army*, commanded by Von Kluck. It invaded Belgium on 13 August and entered France on 24 August, having passed through Vise, Hasselt, Aerschot and Laeken. After fighting at Soissons and Beauvraignes, it was transported to the Wytschaete-Messines district at the beginning of November. At the end of the month it was sent to Russia.

3 Bavarian

Recruited in the Bavarian Palatinate, along with *4 Bavarian Division*, it constituted *II. Bavarian Army Corps* in the *Sixth Army*. After fighting at the Battle of Morhange it moved to the Somme, pillaging Gerbeviller on the way. After fighting in the Peronne area it was transported to Flanders where it re-joined *Sixth Army*. From November 1914 until October 1915, it and its parent corps held the front from the Ypres-Comines canal as far as Douve. During this period it was mostly used as a defensive division.

4 Infantry

The division was raised in Pomerania and detrained at Rheydt near Mönchengladbach on 9 and 10 August before moving into Belgium on 14 August. By 25 August the division was fighting in France. It did not return to Belgium until late in 1917.

4 Bavarian

Recruited in Lower Franconia, after fighting in Lorraine and on the Somme, the division was sent to the south of Ypres towards the end of October. It served in the sector of Wytschaete from November through to October 1915 as a defensive unit. Captured notebooks recorded the heavy losses the division had taken: 9 November *5 Bavarian Infantry Regiment* had been reduced to less than 800 men.

4 Ersatz

The division was organised in August 1914, by grouping together brigade *Ersatz Battalions* from the Third, Fourth and Ninth districts (Brandenburg Prussian-Saxony, Mecklenburg, Schleswig-Holstein and Hansa towns). After serving in Lorraine, where the division fought on the Marne-Rhine Canal, it suffered heavy losses at Mazerulles and fought in the attack on Nancy. The division entrained on 23 September for Brussels, arriving on 25 September. From there it went to Bruges on 11 October, moving to Ostend on 16 October. It then went into the line in front of the Belgians on the right bank of the Yser during November.

5 Reserve

Formed as part of *III. Reserve Corps*, the division, consisted of reservists from the Brandenburg area, was part of First Army and entered Belgium on 18 August after detraining at Crefeld between 10 and 12 August. The division was at Malines on 22 August and Vilvorde four days later, where it fought against the Belgians. Its parent corps then turned towards Antwerp which it besieged before moving toward the sea through Ghent and Bruges between 13 and 16 October. The division attacked in the direction of Nieuport on 19 October and by the beginning of November was fighting in the vicinity of Bixschoote, in Houthulst Forest; then, until the end of November, it held the Dixmude-Langemarck front, before entraining for the Eastern Front.

6 Bavarian Reserve

Recruited in the 1st and 2nd Bavarian recruiting districts, the division was formed in September and sent to Belgium around 21 October. It was sent towards Dadizeele on 27 October and two days later was in Gheluvelt but did not take part in the fighting. On

1 November it took up positions between Hollebeke and Messines and the next day 'attacked in the direction of Wytschaete suffering heavy losses'; from a strength of around two hundred officers and men, '*3 Company* of *21 Reserve Regiment* was reduced to three provisional officers and sixty-three men.'

6 Reserve

Recruited in Brandenburg, the division was part of III. Reserve Corps which formed part of First Army under General von Kluck. It entered Belgium on 17 August, passed through Belgian Limburg and moved on to Malines to face the Belgian offensive. On 9 September, the division attacked the Belgian troops in the region of Louvain and then took part in the siege of Antwerp.

After the fall of Antwerp it followed the same route as *5 Reserve* and by 19 October concentrated near Thourout before fighting on the Yser canal. It fought violently in the region of Nieuport-Dixmude at the end of October and the beginning of November. At the beginning of December *III. Reserve Corps* was sent to Russia. It never returned to Flanders.

9 Reserve

Along with *10 Reserve Division*, the division formed part of *V. Reserve Corps* in *Fifth Army*. After fighting in France the division was sent to Flanders about 13 November. Some of its units fought at Poelcapelle and south of Bixschoote in support of III *Reserve Corps,* suffering heavy casualties. During December the division returned to Woevre in France.

13 Infantry

From the *VII. Corps* district of Westphalia, the division was part of *Second Army*. It entrained at Eupen between 9 and 11 August and one of its brigades took part in the final stage of the siege of Liège. After the fall of Liège the division moved to France and never returned to Flanders.

14 Infantry

With *13 Division* it formed part of *VII. Corps*. Its *27 Brigade* (from Cologne) fought at Liège with five different brigades from five different corps before the remainder of the division joined it on 13 August. Shortly after the fall of Liège the division was sent to France and did not return to Belgium.

14 Reserve

With *13 Reserve Division,* it formed part of *VII. Reserve Corps*. It was formed from the reserve brigade at Senne camp and the surplus *28 Brigade* from *14 Infantry Division.* One regiment from the latter brigade, *39 Fusiliers* from Dusseldorf, appeared in front of Liège on 8 August while the rest of the division was being assembled at Dueren. The remainder of the division entered Belgium on 16 August as part of *Second Army* and fought at Namur and then Maubege. On 10 September it was sent to strengthen the Aisne front and did not return to Belgium.

15 Infantry

The division was formed from men of the Aix-la-Chapelle, Cologne and Bonn area and was part of *VIII. Corps* in the Duke of Württemberg's *Fourth Army. 25 Regiment* was detached and used at the siege of Liège while the remainder of the division entered Belgium on 19/20 August going into action on 22 and 23 August before entering France on 26 August. It did not return to Belgium until late in September 1917.

15 Reserve

Recruited in the Rhine Province and manned throughout the war by recruits from the region, *15 Reserve Division* entered Belgium as part of *VIII. Reserve Corps* in *Fourth Army* on 21 August, fighting at Maissin on 22 August and Paliseul; between 25 and 27 August it crossed the Meuse near Sedan, losing heavily. By 28 August the second battalion of *69 Reserve Infantry* Regiment had been reduced to 140 men. The division was transferred to France and did not return to Belgium.

16 Reserve

On 14 August the division entered Luxemburg on 21 August before fighting in Belgium on 22 August at St. Hubert and at Matton on 24 August. It crossed the Meuse at Sedan with heavy losses between 26 and 28 August. The division was raised in the Rhine Province and formed part of *VIII. Reserve Corps* in *Fourth Army.* It did not return to Belgium.

17 Infantry

Upon mobilisation, *17 Division* with *18 Division,* formed *IX. Corps* (Schleswig-Holstein and Mecklenburg). It gave *81 Brigade* to the new *17 Reserve Division* in *9 Reserve Corps.*

  The division formed part of *First Army* and on 3 August it sent one of its Brigades, *34 Mecklenburg,* to Liège, where it was rejoined by its reservists and by the other brigade, *33 Hanseatic* between 9 and 13 August. On 20 August the division was at Louvain, and on 24 August went into action against British troops. It went around Maubege on 25 August and went to France. The division did not return to Belgium until late July 1917.

17 Reserve

Upon its formation, of recruits from Schleswig-Holstein and the Hanseatic cities, the division was used to guard the coast of Schleswig-Holstein. Entraining on 23 August it was at Louvain on 25 August, at Brussels from 30 August until 3 September. It reached Termonde on 4 September where it encamped until 9 September when it was rushed to France. It did not return to Belgium until late in 1916.

18 Division

From *IX. Corps* district of Schleswig-Holstein, at the outbreak of the war the division formed part of *First Army* . It entrained at Aix-la-Chapelle between 8 and 10 August and was at Liège on 13 August. It went into action at Tirlemont on 18 August, at Mons on 23 August, entering France on 25 August where it fought for the next two years.

18 Reserve

Like *18 Infantry Division,* it was from Schleswig-Holstein and was used to guard the local coast until 22 August when it entrained for Belgium. Advancing rapidly it helped take and then sack Louvain on 25 August, occupied Hamme on 1 September and went to

Termonde on 4 September. On 9 September it was rushed to France and did not return to Belgium until late 1916.

19 Infantry

Raised in Hanover and the Duchy of Oldenburg, along with *20 Division,* it constituted *X. Corps,* part of Von Bulow's *Second Army.* On 3 August its *38 Brigade* was at Malmédy and on 5 August joined the attack on Liège. After the fall of Liège the division fought at Charleroi on 23 August, moving to France on 25 August. The division did not return to Belgium.

19 Reserve

Recruited in Hanover, the Grand Duchy of Oldenburg and the Duchy of Brunswick, the division, along with *2 Reserve Guard Division* formed *X. Corps* that entered Belgium, via Spa on 15 August. It went into action at Nalinnes on 23 August before entering France on 26 August. It did not return to Belgium until late in 1917.

20 Infantry

As part of *X. Corps,* it entered Belgium on 11 August and fought at Charleroi before moving to France. It did not return to Belgium until late in 1917.

21 Infantry

Along with *25 Division*, it formed *XVIII. Corps* and was recruited in Hesse-Nassau, Hesse-Hombourg and Frankfurt. After entering Belgium on 10 August as part of *Fourth Army,* it fought on 20 August at Neufchâteau, and two days later it was in action at Bertrix and Orgeo. It left for France the next day and did not return to Belgium.

21 Reserve

With *25 Reserve Division* it was recruited in Hesse-Nassau and the south of Westphalia. It formed part of *XVIII. Reserve Corps* in the Prince of Württemberg's *Fourth Army,* crossing into Belgium at Martelange around 12 August. After fighting at Neufchâteau on 22 August the division was sent to France and did not return.

22 Infantry

Raised in the Electorate of Hesse as part of *XI. Army Corps* based at Cassel, the division sent *43 Brigade* to Liège between 2 and 3 August. After the fall of the city, the division went to Namur before proceeding to Russia. It never returned to Belgium.

22 Reserve

IV. Reserve Corps, part of *First Army,* comprised *7* and *22 Reserve Divisions.* It was recruited in the Electorate of Hesse and in Thuringia. The division served briefly in Brussels before leaving for France. It returned to Belgium in early 1918.

23 Infantry

Raised in Saxony as part of *XII. Army Corps* in *Second Army,* it arrived in Belgium on 18 August and went into action at Dinant on 23 August, crossed the Meuse the next day and moved into France on 26 August. It did not return to Belgium.

25 Infantry
The division, recruited in the Grand Duchy of Hesse, was also known as the *Hessian Grand Ducal Division*. As part of *XVIII. Army Corps,* it entered Belgium on 19 August, fought at Maissin on 22 August and entered France two days later. It returned to Belgium in late 1917.

25 Reserve
Part of *XVIII. Reserve Corps* in *Fourth Army*, the division originated in the Grand Duchy of Hesse and the Electorate of Hesse. Two days after arriving in Belgium it was in action at Neufchâteau on 22 August, at Tremblois the next day and crossed the Meuse on 28 August. It did not return to Belgium.

26 Infantry
From Württemburg, the division was part of *XVIII. Army Corps* in *Fifth Army*. After service in France, the division was sent to Flanders where it took part in the Messines attack of 31 October. After a month in Belgium the division was sent to Russia.

30 Infantry
Raised in Alsace the division formed part of *XV. Army Corps* based in Strasburg and fought in France in the early part of the war. As part of *Sixth Army,* it went into action south east of Ypres in October 1914 where it remained for over a year.

32 Infantry
At the start of the war *32* and *23 Infantry Divisions* formed *XII. Army Corps (1 Saxon Army Corps)*. Entering Belgium on 13 August with *3 Army,* it fought near Dinant before advancing into France.

38 Infantry
At the start of the war, *38 Division* , raised in the Thuringian States, formed part of *XI. Army Corps* in *Third Army* which went through the Belgian Ardennes to Namur. After the city surrendered, the division was sent to East Prussia and did not return to the Flanders front until late in 1916.

38 Landwehr Brigade
An independent brigade originating from Hanover, the brigade arrived at Liège on 21 October and remained there for about two months before moving to the sector north of the Passchendaele Canal near Nieuport. After occupying the front of Ypres near Beclaere, the brigade went into the line near Passchendaele at the end of December.

40 Infantry
Also known as *4 Saxon Division,* it formed part of *XIX. Army Corps* with *24 Infantry Division (2 Saxon Division)*. The division passed through Belgium on 18 August to fight in France. At the beginning of October its parent corps was transferred to Lille. Attacked by the British, it was forced back upon the line between Ploegsteert Wood and Grenier Wood.

43 Reserve

The division was formed in October, and with *44 Reserve Division,* became *XXII. Reserve Corps.* It was formed from the regimental recruit depots of the *Guards* who were of a high standard; selective recruiting from the whole of Prussia allowed it to maintain a high standard of personnel. By 19 October the division was fighting in the vicinity of Dixmude, Merckem and Bixschoote and continued to be engaged there until the end of November.

After the battle of the Yser, the division occupied various parts of the front between Ypres and Nieuport.

44 Reserve

Formed in Brandenburg between August and October, the division was part of *XXII. Reserve Corps* with *43 Reserve Division.* Detraining at Termonde, it was in action at Dixmude and at Bixschoote in October and November, and lost very heavily. On 9 November, *3 Battalion* of *205 Reserve Infantry Regiment* was reduced to 153 men.

After the Yser battle it was in the line in several sectors north of Ypres.

45 Reserve

A Pomeranian division, *45 Reserve,* was raised between August and October. By 21 October, it was engaged in the battle of the Yser in the vicinity of Noordschoote-Steenstraat, and suffered serious losses. The official casualty lists for the period 15 October to 11 November show fifty two officers and 1,669 men dead or wounded.

In December the division was in the line around Bixschoote.

Wir halten sie fern von den heimischen Fluren

Reserve-Infanterie-Regt. Nr. 233

Many Infantry regiments had their own postcards printed to send home. This card, from Rudolph Fleischmann, a soldier in *233 Reserve Infantry Regiment* in *51 Reserve Infantry Division*, was sent to his family just before Christmas. The division had fought at Langemarck and continued to serve in the vicinity until sent to Russia in 1916.

46 Reserve

Recruited in the Hanseatic cities and Grand Duchy of Mecklenburg, the division, along with *45 Reserve Division*, was part of *XXIII Reserve Corps.* After training, the division entrained for Belgium on 12 October and was in action on the Yser between Dixmude and Bixschoote on 21 October. During the battles of October and November the division suffered heavily. By 21 November only one officer remained in *3 Battalion* of *214 Reserve Infantry Regiment*, and *11 Company*, which started with 253 men, had only ninety left.

After the battle, the division occupied the area around Bixschoote.

51 Reserve

Created between August and October, the division raised its personnel from Thuringia and the Electorate of Hesse. As part of *XXVI. Reserve Corps*, the division went into action northeast of Ypres in the middle of October and was fighting between Cortemarck and Moorslede by 22 October, reaching Langemarck on 24 October.

52 Reserve

Raised in the Rhine Province between August and October, the division, as part of *XXVI. Reserve Corps,* left for Belgium on 12 October and was engaged in the first battle of Ypres around 22 October, fighting around Langemarck and Passchendaele and suffering heavy casualties. Between 18 and 28 October, *240 Reserve Infantry Regiment* listed casualties of twenty eight officers and 1,360 men.

A considerable number of the newly formed divisions in 1914 contained war volunteers. This artist drawn card shows *242 Reserve Infantry Regiment* of *53 Reserve Division (Saxony)* in the attack. The division lost heavily during First Ypres.

53 Reserve

As part of *XXVII. Reserve Corps,* the division was raised in Saxony at the start of the war and was sent to Belgium in October. It was engaged against the British during the first battles around Ypres, fighting between Poelcapelle and Becelaere around 21 October, south east of Gheluvelt on 29 October and near the Ypres-Menin Road at the time of the great attack of 11 November. It suffered very heavy losses: *25 Reserve Chasseurs Battalion,* already reduced to 225 men on 31 October, had only seventy three by 4 November. On 25 November, *6 Company* of *241 Reserve Infantry Regiment* had only seven of the men left who constituted it upon its departure from Saxony.

54 Reserve

The division was formed of men from Württemburg with one regiment and one battalion from Saxony. Its first action was at Ypres on 21 October and on 29 of the month it made an unsuccessful attack south of Gheluvelt. Moving north, it fought at Zonnebeke during the general attack of 11 November where it lost heavily. Between 21 October and 20 November, *248 Reserve Infantry Regiment* listed thirty-two officers and 1,395 men as casualties.

The effect of a 42cm shell on the entrance of Fort Wavre Ste. Catherine.

Infantry halting in front of Antwerp town hall on their way to the front.

A gun taken at Maubege on duty at Middelkerke.

The German General Commissioner for Belgian banks, Dr. Carl von Lumm (in the centre) with assistant staff (from left to right): Dr. Schacht, Manager of the Dresden Bank, Dr. Gutleben from the Darmstadt Bank, Dr. Somari and Prince George of Sachsen-

Professor Captain Lepsius (a doctor) on the left poses with Soeurs de la Providence in the convent gardens.

Belgian POWs in Malines being guarded by a solitary marine. An officer poses with the group.

Belgian POWs taken at Antwerp pose with their guard in Mecheln on their way to a prison camp.

Lightly guarded British POWs are marched back to a railhead for transit to their new accommodation in Germany.

Captured Belgian fortress guns from the citadel in Lüttich.

The Cloth Hall was one of the largest commercial buildings of the Middle Ages, when it served as the main market and warehouse for the Flemish city's prosperous cloth industry. Here it is pictured before the war.

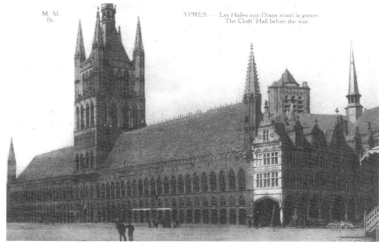

Heavily escorted British POWs. The original caption noted that they were clothed in neat and practical field uniforms.

The original wartime caption states that the picture shows a captured Colonel leading his men through Amerika village near Wervik.

Midday concert in Bruges market-place provided by a German Army band.

Left: The remains of a turret in Loncin fort at Lüttich.

Right: The defences at Lüttich were no match for the 42 cm howitzers used by the German Army.

The result of a direct hit on the Hotel Littoral in Ostend. Because of the naval bombardment, German Naval officers moved to the Hotel de la Couronne. Strict blackout came into force and only guards were allowed out on the front at night.

Soldiers pose outside a house in Malines damaged during the September bombardment of the city.

The Dutch frontier station at Putte on the road to Bergen op Zoon.

The German
Governor General
for Belgium
inspecting the
electrified barbed
wire at the Dutch
border near Limburg.

Troops pose on the
roof of Fort Loncin
at Lüttich. The photo
clearly shows the
damage caused by
the heavy mortars.

The destruction
caused by shells from
Fat Bertha on the
Fort Ste. Catherine
at Antwerp.

The entrance to Fort Talaert.

Destroyed barbed wire entanglements and barricades in front of fort Loncin at Lüttich.

A food column crossing the Grand Place in Antwerp.

Generalfeldmarschall Freiherr von der Goltz was appointed military governor of Belgium at the outbreak of the war. He dealt ruthlessly with what remained of Belgian resistance to German occupation, mostly sniper-fire and damaging rail and telegraph lines. "It is the stern necessity of war that the punishment for hostile acts falls not only on the guilty, but on the innocent as well…In the future, villages in the vicinity of places where railway and telegraph lines are destroyed will be punished without pity (whether they are guilty or not of the acts in question). With this in view hostages have been taken in all villages near the railway lines which are threatened by such attacks. Upon the first attempt to destroy lines of railway, telegraph or telephone, they will immediately be shot."

Hitler praised Goltz's actions and in September 1941 linked Nazi atrocities in Eastern Europe with those in Belgium during World War I.

'The old Reich knew already how to act with firmness in the occupied areas. That's how attempts at sabotage to the railways in Belgium were punished by Count von der Goltz. He had all the villages burnt within a radius of several kilometres, after having had all the mayors shot, the men imprisoned and the women and children evacuated.'

The ruins of the city of Louvain showing the destruction caused by the mass burnings of 25 to 30 August by German troops. 'For five consecutive days the city was burnt and looted. Its library of ancient manuscripts was burnt and destroyed, as was Louvain's university (along with many other public buildings). The church of St. Pierre was similarly badly damaged by fire. Citizenry of Louvain were subject to mass shootings, regardless of age or gender.'

Automobile column outside the offices of the German commander of Lüttich and district.

The inside of a fort at Lüttich.

Anti-aircraft protection on a hotel roof on the sea front near Ostend.

To protect against a possible British landing, Marines dug into the dunes along the coast. This photo shows German light infantry manning machine gun positions facing Belgian positions.

The western end of the dining room at The Majestic Hotel, in Ostend, seen from the street. A naval shell had crashed through the upper part of the window.

Troops making their way to the front.

Troop column marching to Ghent and the channel.

A Petty Officer and ratings on a street corner in Ostend.

A column of marines using captured Belgian dog carts to pull machine guns and supplies.

A Marine on the pontoon ferry at Antwerp.

Privy Councillor von Lumm standing near the hole made by a 42cm shell in one of Antwerp's forts.

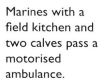

Marines with a field kitchen and two calves pass a motorised ambulance.

The myriad of military clothes and equipment left by the retreating Belgian troops in Antwerp; materiel intended to equip newly called-up recruits.

The citadel of Namur in more peaceful times.

Notices pasted to a wall in newly captured Namur.

The German navy installed numerous coastal batteries along the coast as defence against invasion and the Royal Navy coming too close to shore. The photo shows a naval plotting office.

Naval officers and ratings pose beside one of the guns of Leutnant Haag's battery. On the left are Kapitanleutnant Bess and, in army uniform, Leutnant Haag.

A gun crew getting ready to fire on a British torpedo boat.

Small calibre rapid fire gun in the dunes as a defence against intruding small ships and any potential landing craft.

Belgian refugees in Holland read the hand written messages left by other refugees in the hope of finding friends and relatives.

Refugees returning to Antwerp from Holland.

A field post station set up in Stenay during the August advance.

The Kaiser in full dress uniform at the start of the war.

The town square at Lombardzyke near Ypres.

General von Beseler, commander of *III Reserve Corps* whose troops invested and took Antwerp.

General von Kluck, commander of *First Army* that invaded Belgium in August 1914.

German troops outside Antwerp town hall.

Map of the Western Front showing the movements of the seven armies attacking in France and Belgium.

A wounded officer on a stretcher is placed upon a cart for transportation to the rear.

How the home front saw the war. The enemy would quickly be beaten: 'what's German doesn't retreat. A lot of enemy, a lot of honour.'

The original caption read 'Only seven more Kilometres to Ypres'.

Wounded British troops resting in a café at Roubaix after their capture near Ypres.

The ruins of an armoured turret in Fort Wavre St. Catherine in Antwerp; the result of a direct hit by a 42cm mortar shell. This card was sent by a soldier in *XII Reserve Corps*, a unit that fought in Belgium in the first weeks of the war before moving to France.

Der Drei-Verband.

Comines is located at the Franco-Belgian border, and is split into two parts: Comines (France) and Comines (Belgium), part of the municipality of Comines-Warneton. The belfry of Comines is listed as a UNESCO World Heritage Site.

A pun on the word verband – bandage/alliance. The Triple Entente is bandaged together because they have been wounded by the German Army.

Another mass-produced postcard for the Home Front showing the destruction wrought upon a fort at Lüttich.

In the Allied press, the German soldier was branded as a barbarian and accused of numerous atrocities. In response the Home Front countered with their version of the behaviour of their soldiers in occupied territory. Here the German 'barbarian' demonstrates his cooking skills to an appreciative female audience.

A painting by Professor Schulze of Berlin showing the use of an observation balloon as an artillery spotter somewhere on the Western Front. The British Army did not use them until 1915 and so was at a disadvantage when it came to observing their artillery fire.

A French postcard of the shell damage to Nieuport church, sent by a French soldier to his wife. On the reverse he described the projectiles that passed overhead, coming from large Austrian guns, and how one shell destroyed a whole house.

Collection point for troops waiting to be ferried across the River Schelde; British troops had blown the bridges.

A 10 Pfennig art card sold to raise funds for soldiers invalided out of the army; three Pfennig of the cost went to the charity. Heavy artillery is firing on Ypres during a night shoot using a searchlight to aid observation; possibly an artist's flight of imagination.

An artist's portrayal of the capture of Lüttich.

A New Year's card from an officer serving in Munich to his friend, a captain in *Reserve Artillery Regiment 53*, in *XXVII Reserve Corps* of *53 Reserve Division* serving north of Ypres. 'With God for King and Country', the card was sent from Bavaria, a semi-independent country within the German State that had its own King.

An unidentified soldier poses prior to departing for the front.

A mobile 21cm mortar unit defending the Belgian coast against Royal Naval intrusion. The shell's trajectory was aimed at hitting the warship's deck where the armour was at its thinnest.

General von Emmich on the East Front with the Kaiser. Emmich was the 'commander of the Maas Army (Army of the Meuse), a 60,000 strong task force assigned to conduct the initial engagement of the Great War, a 10-day battle for the fortress town of Liège. Von Emmich successfully led this six brigade, three cavalry division-strong reinforced detachment as they systematically took out Liege's twelve fortresses and main citadel. For this effort, he became the first German soldier during the war to receive the coveted Pour le Merite award.' Accepting the surrender of the Liège garrison by its commander Lt. General Leman, he told the general, "You have nobly protected your forts. Keep your sword...to have crossed swords with you has been an honour, sir."

'Following the siege, von Emmich resumed command of his *X.Army Corps*, carrying out operations near Reims until April 1915. He and his corps were then sent to Galicia on the Eastern Front, where they fought with General von Mackensen and were successfully engaged in battles at Gorlice-Tarnow and the Fortress of Lemberg. In early autumn of 1915, von Emmich became ill in the field and was replaced as *X.Army Corps* commander by General Walter von Lüttwitz. He returned to Germany to recuperate but succumbed to his sickness, dying on 22 December 1915 in Hanover.'

After Lüttich had fallen and the battle moved on most of the troops in the city were the more elderly, responsible for garrison duties. The area was obviously thought to be safe as none of the troops are carrying rifles or side arms as they walk through the town.

19 October 1914. A soldier decorated with flowers stands in front of the rifles and packs of the remainder of his unit.

An officer off to the front. Unlike enlisted men they were provided with a carriage with seats. Enlisted men often travelled by wagon.

A card sent by a soldier in *I Bavarian Reserve Jägerbataillon of 5 Bavarian Reserve Division* in April 1916 while he was serving in the Artois region. The photo shows the bridge at Namur destroyed by the retreating Belgians on 26 August 1914.

Six members of *13 Reserve Infantry Regiment* prior to leaving for the front. *13 Reserve Infantry Division*, in which they fought, was about to leave for Belgium where it was to be deployed against Maubeuge.

Posted by a soldier in Field Hospital at Tournai the card shows an artist's impression of the village fighting that took place in Belgium at the start of the war.

Original Aufnahme vom Kriegsschauplatz.
Das einsame Grab eines Garde Dragoners
auf dem Fort Loucin bei Lüttich; der Tapfere
fiel bei dem Versuch, die erste Fahne aufzupflanzen.

A soldier poses next to the lonely grave of the Dragoon Guard who planted the flag on Fort Loucin at Lüttich.

Die Brücke über die Maas
bei Dun

German Army
transport wagons
crossing the River
Maas during the
advance.

German marines
parading through
Mecheln shortly after
its capture.

Original-Aufnahme
vom westlichen Kriegsschauplatz
Deutsche Marinesoldaten in Mecheln

Kr 133 b
Verlag von
GUSTAV LIERSCH & C?
BERLIN S.W.

Schützengräben u. Unterstände in den Dünen.

To protect against
invasion, the coastal
regions had to be
defended. This
photograph clearly
shows the size of
the trench system in
the dunes.

Albrecht, Duke of Württemberg, 'commanded the German *4th Army* and led them to victory in the Battle of the Ardennes in August 1914. Following this victory, the *4th Army* saw action in the First Battle of the Marne before being transferred to Flanders in October, where Duke Albrecht commanded them during the Battle of the Yser. Duke Albrecht also commanded the German forces during the Second Battle of Ypres, where poison gas was used on a large scale for the first time.'

A frieze, based on Romano/ Greek art, of the bitter- sweetness of the departure for the front.

Der Hauptmann er lebe er geht uns kühn voran
Wir folgen ihm mutig auf blut'ger Siegesbahn
Er führt uns jetzt zum Kampf und Sieg hinaus
Er führt uns einst ihr Brüder ins Vaterhaus

A romantic view of the entry of German troops into Belgium.

An artist's impression of the joy experienced by troops leaving for the front with flowers and messages.

A card celebrating the capture of Antwerp and the equipment used to take it. General von Beseler was the victorious commander of *III.Reserve Corps.*

Very quickly it became the People's War. An artist's depiction of the capture of a French field gun.

Beschießung von Ypern durch deutsche Artillerie.

Aircraft were used from the very start of the war to assist the artillery. This is an artist's impression of a spotter plane assisting the German artillery during its shelling of Ypres.

Sammeln der Truppen am Abend nach der Schlacht bei Ypern.

An artist's impression of troops massing for an evening attack on Ypres.

An armed medic, contrary to the Geneva Convention. Both soldiers are wearing the Mannschaftskoppelschloß 1895 – 1915 (Belt buckle) used by troops from state of Hesse. *25 Infantry Division* served in Belgium around the time this photo was taken.

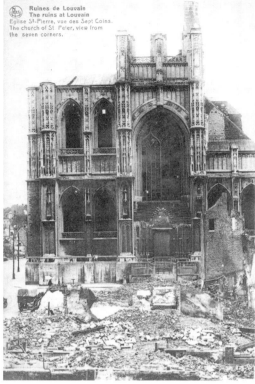

A view of the destruction caused to the church of St. Peter during the burning of Louvain.

It was not until the battle had moved on that photos were available to celebrate the fall of the fortress towns of Belgium. This is an artist's impression of the capture of a fort in Namur.

With the speed of the advance it was not always easy for the artillery to keep up with the infantry, particularly over rough terrain. Such rapid advances were hard on the horses.

Retribution was harsh during the advance when franc-tireurs were involved. This shows the Rue des Tanneurs in Dinant; twenty-eight inhabitants were shot here on 23 August by Saxon troops.

A newly built wood framed blockhouse in Westflanders.

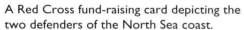

Zwei Seelen und ein Gedanke!

GENERAL v. BESELER

GEORG BERGER
1915

Ob in Belgien oder ostwärts Kadinen:
Spezialist in Festungsruinen!

A Red Cross fund-raising card depicting the two defenders of the North Sea coast.

General von Beseler who was left behind the main German thrust to invest Antwerp. He was later transferred to the Eastern Front.

Railways were the quickest method of moving troops, guns and supplies to the front so considerable manpower was used to repair and maintain them.

Feldskizze.   *Gefecht bei Tirlemont (Belgien.)*

An artist's impression of the capture of Tirlemont from the French on 19 August.

A propaganda song card. A misty eyed-view of troops moving off to the war.

The ruins of the church in Termonde after it had been burned.

An artist's impression of the fighting on the Yser depicting French Grenadiers attacking German positions.

On both sides reservists were called up before the war. When war was declared in Belgium many men who had not previously served were also called up and quickly trained. In this photo a Belgian General is passing in review new recruits as they leave for the front.

GÉNÉRAL BELGE PASSANT EN REVUE
LES NOUVELLES RECRUES PARTANT AU FRONT
A Belgian General passing in review the new recruits starting for the front

The War. — A divine service in a belgian church. — While the inhabitants pray, the soldiers repose on the straw. — LL.

Business as usual for this church. While a Belgian soldier sleeps in the straw, the local inhabitants carry on with their morning service.

An artist's impression of the surrender of the Prussian Guard to the Middlesex Regiment during a failed attack at Ypres during December.

An Allied propaganda card showing the litter caused by German troops drinking in the streets.

Another idealised version of life at the front. A Red Cross fund raising card for the wounded, sold for ten Pfennig with three Pfennig going to the charity.

A Belgian soldier poses fully armed and ready to fight using his FN Mauser rifle.

A sergeant in a reserve regiment poses before departure for the front.

Many towns suffered like Louvain. This picture shows the damage to the church in Vise.

Belgian soldiers of the 2nd Regiment smile for the camera.

Just one of the 11,100 wagons taking over 3,000,000 men and 860,000 horses to war.

A reservist in Landau poses for his photo prior to leaving for the front.

Reiterpatrouille in Flandern.

Cavalry were often sent ahead of the main body of troops to act as scouts. An artist's impression of the loneliness of such a patrol.

Ruines de Louvain
The ruins at Louvain

Entrée de la rue de Namur.
Beginning of the Namur street.

Namur street in Louvain showing the destruction caused during the ransacking of the city.

Strafe muss sein!

GRUSS AUS DER KRIEGSSCHULE.

Political humour likening the Allied nations to naughty boys who needed punishing. 'Greetings from the War School'

A memorial, erected by German troops, commemorates the deaths of soldiers on both sides at Mons.

Inspecting a shot down German Taube aircraft on the Yser front. Note the armoured car and mobile anti-aircraft gun on the road.

A German heavy mortar captured by the French in the early days of the campaign.

A Belgian soldier stands in the ruins of Malines.

No rush to get your beating. In turn the German Army will spank you.

While maintaining strict neutrality, the Dutch army was mobilised and ready for war. A photo taken of Dutch troops resting in Utrecht. The Dutch government mobilized 500,000 men 'to reinforce the regular army. They guarded the borders and filled their days with exercising and polishing.'

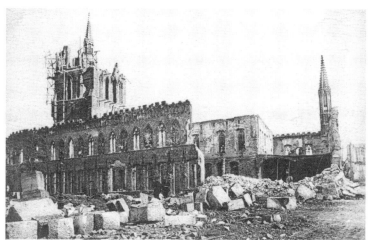

The Cloth Hall in flames and after the fire was put out.

Gunners take a break while awaiting orders. Their field gun is camouflaged to avoid detection by enemy planes and the resultant counter-battery fire that would result if spotted.

A British postcard of the damage done to the Cathedral in Malines during the bombardment. The caption reads 'On Sept 1st 73 shells were fired into the unfortified town of Malines, Belgium, by the Germans. Much damage was done to the Cathedral and other historic buildings. The valuable stained glass windows were smashed and many rare and priceless pictures destroyed.'

Troops marching through Blankenberge.

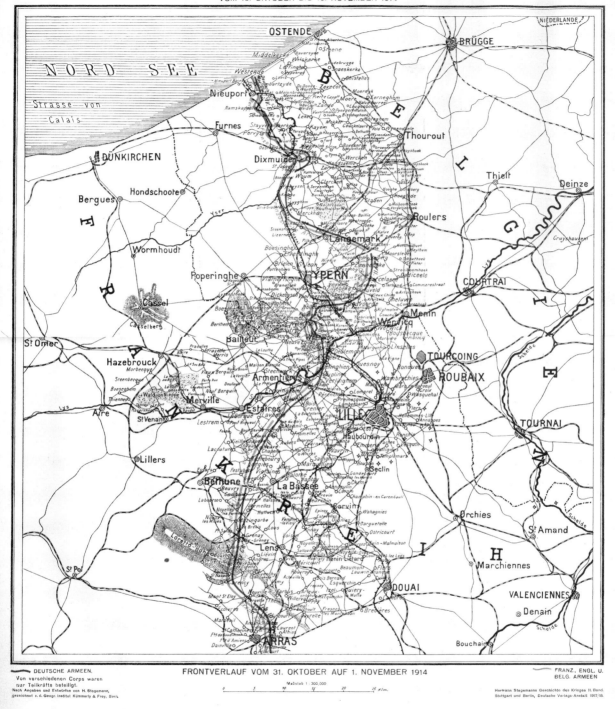

FRONTVERLAUF VOM 31. OKTOBER AUF 1. NOVEMBER 1914

A German map showing the front in Flanders at the end of October 1914. The term Flanders was not synonymous with modern day Flanders – it covered a wider area.

The original caption for this photograph read: 'The German colony in Westend village with communication trench in the foreground.'

Bibliography

Baer. C H. Der Völkerkrieg – Erster Band. Julius Hoffmann. 1914.

Baer. C H. Der Völkerkrieg – Zweiter Band. Julius Hoffmann. 1914.

Baer. C H. Der Völkerkrieg – Siebenter Band. Julius Hoffmann. 1916.

Baer. C H. Der Völkerkrieg – Zehnter Band. Julius Hoffmann. 1916.

Beckett, I.F.W. Ypres The first battle. Pearson, 2004.

Binding, R. A Fatalist at war. George Allen & Unwin. 1933.

Bull, S. German Assault troops of the First World War. Spellmount. 2007.

Chickering, R. Imperial Germany and the Great War, 1914–1918. Cambridge University Press, 2005.

Dewar, M. The First Flame Attacks. Volume 3 History of the First World War. Purnell, 1971.

Edmonds, Brigadier General Sir James, CB, CMG. Military Operations France & Belgium1914, volume 1. Macmillan & Co, 1922.

Edmonds, Brigadier General Sir James, CB, CMG. Military Operations France & Belgium1914, volume 2. Macmillan & Co, 1925.

Edmonds, Brigadier General Sir James, CB, CMG. Military Operations France & Belgium 1915, volume 1. Macmillan & Co, 1927.

Foley, R. German strategy and the path to Verdun. Cambridge University Press. 2005.

Görlitz, W(ed). The Kaiser and his court (the First World War diaries of Admiral Georg von Müller). Macdonald. 1961.

Gray, R & Argyle, C. Chronicle of the First World War Volume 1, 1914 – 1916. Facts on File, 1991.

Gray, R & Argyle, C. Chronicle of the First World War Volume 2, 1917 – 1921. Facts on File, 1991.

Hedin, S. With the German Armies in the West. John Lane. 1915.

Herwig, H. The First World War, Germany and Austria 1914–1918. Arnold, Headline Group. 1997.

Hölcher, G. Geschichte des Weltkriegs – Erster Band. Hoursch & Bechstedt. 1915.

http://en.wikipedia.org/wiki/Albrecht,_Duke_of_Württemberg

http://www.wwiaviation.com/float-planes_central_powers.html

http://home.comcast.net/~jcviser/aka/emmich.htm

http://www.firstworldwar.com/battles/haelen.htm

http://www.firstworldwar.com/battles/louvain.htm

http://www.greatwar.co.uk/ypres-salient/battles-ypres-salient.htm

http://www.historyonthenet.com/WW1/trenches.htm

http://www.landships.freeservers.com/ww1_hmgs.htm

http://pictureshistory.blogspot.com/2009/12/neutral-netherlands-holland-during-ww1.html

Humphries, M O & Maker, J. (editors) Germany's Western Front: Translations from the German Official History of the Great War. Wilfrid Laurier University Press, 2010.

Ludendorff, General. My War Memories 1914–1918 volume 1. Hutchinson (No Date)

Macdonald, L. The death of innocence. Headline. 1993.

Michelin & Cie. Ypres and the battles for Ypres 1914–1918. Michelin & Cie. 1920.

Nash, D.B. Imperial German Army Handbook. Ian Allan. 1980.

Palmer, S & Wallis, S. A War in Words. Simon & Schuster. 2003.

Passingham, I. All the Kaiser's Men. Sutton Publishing. 2003.

Poseck, M von. The German Cavalry. E S Mittler & Son. 1923.

Roynon, G. Massacre of The Innocents – The Crofton Diaries, Ypres 1914–15. Sutton Publishing. 2004.

Scheer, Admiral R. Germany's High Sea Fleet in the World War. Cassel & Co. 1920.

Schwink, O. Ypres, 1914 (The Battle on the Yser and of Ypres in the Autumn 1914). Constable. 1919

Sheldon, J. The German Army at Ypres 1914. Pen & Sword. 2010.

Sulzbach, H. With the German guns. Leo Cooper. 1973

The Times. Documentary History of the War. Volume 8. The Times Publishing Company. 1919

Thoumin, R. The First World War. Secker & Warburg. 1963.

Tichischwitz, E von. Schlachten des Weltkrieges – Antwerpen 1914. Gerhard Stalling. 1925.

Unknown. Battles of the Ypres Salient. The Great War 1914–1918.

Wegener, G. Der Wall von Eisen und Feuer – Ein Jahr an der Westfront. F A Brockhaus. 1915

Weintraub, S. The remarkable Christmas truce of 1914. Simon & Schuster. 2002.

Westman, S. Surgeon with the Kaiser's Army. William Kimber. 1968.

Williams, J.F. Corporal Hitler and the Great War 1914 – 1918. Frank Cass. 2005.

Witkop, P (Ed.). German students' war letters. Pine Street Books. 2002

www.1914–1918.net/bat1.htm The Battle of Mons

Young, Brigadier P. The Great Retreat. Volume 1, History of the First World War. Purnell. 1969.

Zuber, T. The Mons Myth. The History Press, 2010.